Jackie P   28 9 +2

In TOUCH with GOD

In Touch with GOD

EVERYDAY PRAYERS

Peter Bean

Lutheran Publishing House

Published edition copyright © Lutheran Publishing House 1993

Text copyright © Peter Bean 1993

The Scripture texts indicated by TEV are from the *Good News Bible: Today's English Version*, Australian Text Edition, copyright © 1966, 1971, 1976 American Bible Society, and are used by permission of the Bible Society in Australia.

Scripture quotations marked NIV are from the *Holy Bible, New International Version* ® NIV ® Copyright © 1973, 1978, 1984 by International Bible Society.

Those indicated by NRSV are from the *Holy Bible: New Revised Standard Version* copyright © 1989 the Division of Christian Education, National Council of the Churches of Christ, USA.

Except for brief quotations in critical articles and reviews, this book may not be reproduced in whole or in part by any means without prior written permission of the publisher.

Cover design by Graeme Cogdell

Cover photo: Colour Australia, *Waterfall*, Joseph Meehan.

First printing August 1993

00 99 98 97 96 95 94 93   12 11 10 9 8 7 6 5 4 3 2 1

National Library of Australia
Cataloguing-in-Publication entry
Bean, Peter, 1953– .
   In touch with God.

   Includes indexes.
   ISBN 0 85910 652 7.

   1. Prayers. I. Title.

242.8

Typeset in 10 point Stone Serif

Printed and published by Lutheran Publishing House
205 Halifax Street
Adelaide, South Australia

Introduction

'We'll keep in touch' is often said as a heartfelt farewell. To keep in touch continues a relationship even when the two parties are away from each other. God keeps in touch with us through his word and sacraments, through the loving actions of friends, through the blessings of fellowship, through his creation.

He wants us to keep in touch with him too. We do that in various ways, but particularly through prayer. This selection of prayers is offered to help you keep in touch with God.

Some are general prayers; some are more personal. While some can be prayed as they are, others (perhaps the majority) are meant as starter-prayers — to encourage you to speak to God in your own way with your own words. When we read the Psalms we note that the writers pour out their emotions. They praise God, they weep, they yell at God. They question why and when, they sing for joy, they chant their sorrow. My hope is that this collection of prayers will encourage you and challenge you to keep in touch with God — to sing, to weep, to yell, to question, to praise — no matter how far away or how close to him you think you may be.

Peter Bean
February 1993

Contents

Introduction	6
Section 1	
Morning and evening	8
Reflections on the Lord's Prayer	20
Names and images of God	30
Worship	38
Seasons of the Church Year	47
Fruits of the Spirit	55
Church life	64
Section 2	
Daily work and business	76
Education	83
Communication	90
Transport	99
Mental health	107
Section 3	
Stages of life	116
Leisure and relaxation	138
Nature	149
General	157
Section 4	
Blessings	170
Biblical index	176
Topical index	178

SECTION

1

Morning and evening

To begin the day with Jesus, and to end it in the same way, is one of the great blessings God has given us. Let's take advantage of that.

And there was evening, and there was morning.
Genesis 1 (NIV)

Day 1

Very early on the first day of the week, just after sunrise, they were on their way to the tomb . . .
Mark 16:2 (NIV)

Lord Jesus, may I seek you this morning,
as the women sought you
on that resurrection dawn.
And may I be surprised, as they were.
Let me meet you, the living Lord,
so that my dying thoughts and dead actions
may be transformed
by your power and presence.
Give me life this day, Lord,
and throughout this week. Amen.

On the evening of that first day of the week, when the disciples were together, with the doors locked for fear of the Jews, Jesus came and stood among them and said, 'Peace be with you!' John 20:19 (NIV)

As night falls, Jesus,
surround me with your peace.
During the day there are people and events
that frighten me into denying you,
that cause me to act
as if you had no part in my life.
And so I shut the doors of my life.
Walk through them, Lord,
as you did that evening;
break down the barriers I erect,
and come into my life.
Flood me with your peace,
so that my fear may dissipate,
and my life be lived boldly for you.
Let me rest in your peace tonight, Lord. Amen.

Day 2

Early in the morning, Jesus stood on the shore, but the disciples did not realise that it was Jesus.
John 21:4 (NIV)

How often, Lord, do I not recognise you
in the different moments of my existence?
Forgive me and restore my sight.
This morning be with me, as you always are,
walk beside me, and in front of me,
stand close to me, and behind me.
As I go along this journey of life
with you today,
prevent me from asking: Who are you?*
but give me courage to state boldly:
You, Jesus, are my Lord. Amen.

* John 21:12

But they urged him strongly, 'Stay with us, for it is nearly evening; the day is almost over.' So he went in to stay with them. Luke 24:29 (NIV)

As this day draws to a close, my Lord,
I ask that you would stay with me,
and my family.
Thank you for your protection and guidance
through the day;
for walking alongside us
and providing support when needed.
Now, send a restful sleep,
and keep me safe in your care,
so that I may awaken refreshed,
ready to fulfil the role you have planned for me
in the new day. Amen.

Day 3

In the morning, O Lord, you hear my voice; in the morning I lay my requests before you and wait in expectation. Psalm 5:3 (NIV)

I have to admit, Lord,
I don't always come before you in the morning,
but when I do, I know you do hear my voice;
I know my day is filled with anticipation.
This morning, Lord,
I want to spend time with you,
    sharing my concerns,
    bringing my joys and sorrows,
    laying my plans before you.
And as I do, I look forward to your answers;
to your support; to your rejoicing;
to the subtle changes that you weave
into my daily journey,
so that my plans become your plans,
and my ways are directed to become your ways.
Fill me with expectation,
through your Spirit, Jesus. Amen.

*One of those days Jesus went out to a mountainside
to pray, and spent the night praying to God.*
Luke 6:12 (NIV)

Lord, as I think about this evening,
I consider the things I have done:
the reading, the watching,
the listening, the speaking.
No praying!
And apart from a mumbled word
before my eyelids close,
that's how it is most nights.
Give me discipline to pray regularly;
fill me with excitement at spending time
in communicating with you.
Challenge me to follow your example, Jesus,
and spend time in prayer.
You know there are plenty of topics
I could share.
Spirit of God, enliven me,
fill me with your breath.
Make me so alert that one of these days
I just might attempt to spend
the night praying to you. Amen.

Day 4

Weeping may remain for a night, but rejoicing comes in the morning. Psalm 30:5 (NIV)

Lord, I was worn out last night.
The toils of the day had taken their toll.
I didn't know which way to turn,
or who to turn to.
But you were there, God of comfort;
you were there, God of refreshment.
You came into my life —
not that you weren't there before —
and you gave me rest;
you allowed me a sound sleep,
and this morning I feel alive again.
I'm ready to face the day with you.
I want to rejoice in you,
and this morning is as good a time as any.
Amen.

Then the man and his wife heard the sound of the Lord God as he was walking in the cool of the day, and they hid from the Lord God among the trees of the garden. Genesis 3:8 (NIV)

Thanks, Lord, for trees
and their wide canopy of leaves
that provide shade and shelter
from the heat of the day.
Help me not to use them to hide from you.
When you seek me, give me courage
to come boldly before you,
and acknowledge the wrong things
I have done,
and the wrong thoughts I have had;
and just as boldly to seek your charity,
and so be restored into your presence,
through your Son Jesus, who died on a tree
in the heat of the day — for me.
Amen.

Day 5

The steadfast love of the Lord never ceases, his mercies never come to an end; they are new every morning. Lamentations 3:22,23 (NRSV)

Lord God, I delight in watching the sun rise;
in seeing objects take shape
as the darkness is filtered away by the light;
in feeling the warmth of the sun's first rays.
The whole world seems revitalised at that time.
It is new every morning.
And so is your love, and your mercy;
your guiding hand, and your presence,
come to me new every morning.
Thank you, O Lord, for that.
Be present this morning in all your generosity;
inspire and uplift me,
so I may be the person
you have made me — today.
Amen.

At the evening sacrifice, I . . . fell on my knees with my hands spread out to the Lord my God and prayed. Ezra 9:5,6 (NIV)

In this day and age, Lord,
we don't fall on our knees too often.
Teach us again the value
of humbling ourselves.
And pride stops us
from holding out our palms, seeking help.
Shatter our pride;
replace it with soft-heartedness.
I pray to you this evening for a good measure
    of love and peace and joy,
       of kindness and goodness and patience,
       of humility and self-control and faithfulness.
Amen.

Day 6

In the morning you will see the glory of the Lord.
Exodus 16:7 (NIV)

Permit me, Lord, to see your glory today
    in positive conversations,
    in effort in the workplace,
    in family discussion,
    in the splendour of creation,
    in the service of one to another,
    in the joy of living.
And in my activities,
allow me to give glory to you, Lord. Amen.

May my prayer be set before you like incense; may the lifting up of my hands be like the evening sacrifice. Psalm 141:2 (NIV)

Lord, thank you for my senses
and the good things I have received through them:
for the smell of fresh flowers,
and the pleasant fragrance of perfume;
for the taste of the evening meal,
adding to family discussion at the table;
for the sight of trees and creatures
and human creations that give praise to you;
for the hearing of birds in the parks,
and the company of radio programs;
for the touch of a loved one,
and the handshake or hug from a friend.
Lord Jesus, may the use of my senses
give pleasure and praise to you. Amen.

Day 7

I, Jesus . . . am the bright morning star.
Revelation 22:16 (TEV)

I've seen the morning star, Jesus,
strong, like a sentinel.
May you be potent and watchful
in all I do today, Lord.
Shine light into my darkness; guide my footsteps,
so that I am able to negotiate any obstacles.
Influence my decisions through your Holy Spirit.
Guard my actions, so that they may highlight
your presence in my life. Amen.

It will be a unique day, without daytime or nighttime — a day known to the Lord. When evening comes, there will be light. Zechariah 14:7 (NIV)

Lord Jesus, I look forward to this time,
when all that is known to you
will be shared with us all;
when darkness, and its attendant fears,
does not exist;
when daytime is not longed for,
nor so important;
but when all people and things
have their focus on you,
and in you.
Lord Jesus, let your day come —
soon and very soon.
Thank you, Jesus. Amen.

Reflections on the Lord's Prayer

The Lord's Prayer is the ultimate prayer — as taught by Jesus. But it also allows us to direct our thoughts and be guided by the individual phrases.

Our Father

Thanks, God, for loving us with your love,
with your Fatherly love:
perfect and pure,
creative and dynamic,
accepting and forgiving,
refreshing and renewing.
Forgive us when we act as rebellious children.
Draw us back into your love and care. Amen.

God — our Father — you set the example,
but too often we fail you as your representative —
whether father or mother,
teacher or policeman,
boss or whatever authority figure we may be.
Teach us not to use authority as a power base,
but as a way to serve and care and love —
as you show us. Amen.

Father God, work in the hearts of those of us
who have the responsibility and privilege
of being fathers.
Challenge us to act as you act,
    to guide as you guide,

>   to love as you love,
>   to forgive as you forgive,
>   to accept as you accept.
> Make us fathers in your image. Amen.

God, our Father —
for some people *father* is not a pleasant word.
Children don't want to know their father —
and who can blame them
when they've been abused, battered, mistreated,
when all they experience shows them
that *father* is a dirty word.
And yet, Lord God, you are still their Father.
Work through us,
work through all who have contact
with those who have suffered
at the hands of a human father,
so that they may know the love of you —
their heavenly Father,
and may gain
a new understanding and perspective
on the way their true Father works! Amen.

Only God, you are *our* Father —
not mine, but *ours*:
>   to be shared,
>   to be rejoiced in together,
>   to be celebrated as one.
Teach us to live together —
so that our cry may ring true:
'Our Father . . .' Amen.

In heaven

Father God, we hear so many theories
about where heaven is,
or what takes place there.
Reveal to me the reality of heaven.
Draw me close enough to you,
so that I may experience heaven now.*
Keep me faithful to you,
so that I may live in your presence in times to come;
in the name of Jesus,
who ascended into heaven. Amen.

* John 5:24; 11:25

Hallowed be your name

Adonai! Yahweh! I am!
Your name, O God, is holy in itself.

Keep me from using it in less than holy ways.
Let me live in you,
and may you live in me,
so that all my actions and all my words
may give praise to your name.

May your name be made holy in my life,
Lord Jesus. Amen.

Your kingdom come

Kingdoms come and go
throughout history, Lord Jesus,
but yours remains forever.
May I know the dynamics
of your kingdom in my life.
Give me the courage to use the abilities
you have given me
in service to those around me,
so that your love may be known,
and your kingdom may come
into the lives of all whom I have the privilege
of coming into contact with. Amen.

Your will be done

Lord God,
give us the courage to join our prayer
to that of Jesus:
Not my will, but yours be done.*

I thank you, Lord, for the freedom of will
that you have so generously given to me.
Along with this freedom,
give me wisdom and discernment and charity.
When I exercise my will,
allow me to practise justice and mercy,
and live in fellowship with your creation
and you.† Amen.

* Matthew 26:39   † Micah 6:8

On earth, as it is in heaven

In heaven, God, your will reigns supreme.
In the freedom that you have given me,
here on earth,
may your will reign supreme in my life.
Shape me, mould me, bend me,
so that as I experience your love and kindness,
I may, through exercising my will,
extend love and kindness to all around me.
Amen.

Give us today our daily bread

Thank you, God of creation,
for providing all that we need.
I particularly thank you for those things
I so often forget to thank you for.
Thanks for soap, and water,
for toothpaste and deodorant,
for sausages and eggs, for bread and vegemite,
for socks and shoes, and dresses and skirts.

Thanks, God, for rain and sunshine,
for surf and snow,
for plants and trees,
and the garden where I can weed and sow,
for transport and roads, for footpaths and legs.

Provider of all,
continue to provide as you see fit.
Help me to see that I am more than catered for
by your generosity. Amen.

Forgive us our sins

Perfect God,
even though we don't use the word *sin*
so often today,
we still sin in so many ways.

Forgive us, Lord,
when we do not live up to your expectations.

Forgive us, Lord,
when we walk in forbidden places.

Forgive us, Lord,
when we deliberately break your law.

Forgive us, Lord,
when we have contempt for you and defy you.
And as we walk in your forgiveness,
allow us to start anew. Amen.

As we forgive those who sin against us

Lord, it's easy enough to admit my sins to you
and to ask for forgiveness.

But to forgive someone who sins against me —
what do you think I am, God?
Oh, that's right — forgiven!

Lord, as you so freely forgive me,
accept me, and give me a new start,
so enable me to forgive freely,

to accept the one who has offended me,
to make a new start in that relationship —
so that, together,
we may live in forgiveness and peace! Amen.

Lead us not into temptation

Sometimes, Lord, temptations are clear,
and sometimes they are very subtle.

Whatever temptations come,
protect me, guide me, so that
I may walk in your ways, and not mine.

Help me to plan ways of dealing
with those temptations
that are obvious, so that when they come
I may deal with them effectively.

Teach me to rely on you
to resist the subtle temptations,
to call on you for help,
to trust in you for protection.

O Lord, keep me in your care. Amen.

As you resisted temptation, Lord,
so give us strength in you to resist
the temptations that come our way. Amen.

But deliver us from evil

Evil takes many forms, Lord Jesus,
but perhaps can be summed up
in the old formula:
the world, the devil, and self.

Deliver me from the world.
Teach me to be in the world,
but not of the world.
Release me from worldly desires
by letting me know you are all I need
in this world.

Deliver me from the devil.
Let me recognise the reality of the devil,
and the need for your presence and protection.
Thanks, Jesus,
for defeating the devil on the cross.

Deliver me from self.
Take away my anxieties, my fears,
my doubts, my sadness.
Replace them with your compassion, your love,
faith in you, and joy.

Deliver me from evil, Lord,
and let me rest in you. Amen.

For the kingdom, the power, and the glory are yours

Yours, Lord, not mine,
>   not the televangelist's,
>   not the prime minister's or president's,
>   not the sporting hero's,
>   not the devil's,
>   but yours.

May I always acknowledge your power, Lord,
may I always be part of your kingdom.
In all that I do, may I give glory to you. Amen.

Now and forever

Sometimes it's easy, Lord God, to see
that all things will be yours.
Will be! Some time in the future!
At a time when it won't bother me!

But what about *now*?
Lord Jesus, you are the Lord of my life,
and that means now — as well as forever.

May the kingdom, the power, and the glory
that are yours
be present in my life
both now and forever. Amen.

Amen

Your prayer, Lord Jesus,
is a simple, short prayer,
but at the same time encompasses so much.

May my amen be said with vigour
and acted out with conviction,
so that all the things I pray for,
using your words,
and all the thoughts I have
while praying this prayer,
may become a resounding yes to you
and to those around me
through my words and deeds.

As you have taught me to pray,
I pray in your name, Jesus.
Amen.

Names and images of God

The Bible uses many names and pictures of God, all of which reveal a snippet of who God is and what he is like. May these prayers help you to see God a little more clearly.

God the Father

God, Father, teach me what a true Father is like.

Love me, discipline me,
care for me, scold me,
play with me, encourage me,
walk beside me, help me mature,
so that I may lead others to appreciate
and love your fatherliness. Amen.

Abba

God — can I call you Daddy?
It's such an intimate term.
Perhaps I don't want to use it
because I'm scared you'll get too close to me,
and know me too well.
Abba Father — Daddy — let me know the joy
of being in an intimate relationship with you.
Amen.

Mighty God

Mighty God, as I see your awesome power,*
let me rejoice in all the things
you have given me and my family to enjoy. Amen.

* Psalm 66:1–7

Everlasting Father

Lord of history,
be Lord of my life!
God of eternity,
may I know you now,
and in knowing you now,
learn to live with you forever. Amen.

Creator

Lord of creation,
create in me a clean heart.*
Image-maker,
mould me in your image,†
so that I may follow the example
of my Lord Jesus Christ.‡ Amen.

* Psalm 51:10   † Genesis 1:26,27   ‡ Ephesians 5:1,2

God, you have created all things.
Fill me with a sense of awe,
and a willingness to be responsible.

Help me to see you
    in the forests and deserts,
    in the oceans and mountains,
    in the plains and fields,
    in the sky,
    and in the creatures of the earth,
    of the water, of the air.

In my stewardship of these,
let me remember
that you are the maker and owner. Amen.

Lord (Adonai)

Lord, you are in control.
Take control of me,
of my actions and thoughts,
of my relationships and living,
so that you may be Lord of my life.

Adonai, I worship and praise you. Amen.

God the Son

Jesus

Son of God, you took a common name
to remind me that you have become
a common person.

Thank you, Jesus, for your humanness —
for being like me,
for being like those around me.

Remind me constantly
of the things we have in common. Amen.

Christ

And yet, Jesus,
you were the chosen one of God:
the Christ, the promised one.

Allow me to recognise your specialness
and to respect your majesty.
Help me to bear your name with honour.
Amen.

Messiah

Messiah will come!
Messiah has come!
I thank you, Lord,
for coming into the world
and into my life. Amen.

Saviour

Save me, Jesus, from myself
and from my selfish desires.

You are the Saviour of the world,
but you are also my Saviour.
Thanks, Lord,
for your concern and interest in me. Amen.

Redeemer

Some, Jesus,
don't seem to recognise the price you paid.
Help us not to devalue it
by trusting in our selves,
our jobs, our homes, our friends,
ahead of you.
Lord, I praise you for your willingness
to be so generous. Amen.

Immanuel

God with us!
God be with me
>in my walking and talking,
>in my stopping and praying,
>in my running and listening,
>in my reading and sharing,

so that all may see that you, God,
are with me. Amen.

Master

Are you a taskmaster,
or a caring, loving master, Lord?

I know you as a master
who expects responsibility,
but who gives me immense freedom.*
I thank you that you care for me and love me.
Help me to be caring and loving in response.
Amen.

* Galatians 5:1,13–25

Teacher

Teach me your ways, O Lord.*
Help me to learn from you,
so that I may follow your example. Amen.

* Psalm 86:11

Prince of Peace

Prince of peace,
bring your peace into our troubled world.
Rule over your kingdom with authority
and calmness and wisdom.
Let us worship and praise you. Amen.

Son of God

You are the Son of God, Jesus,
and because of you
I am a child of God.
Thank you for welcoming me into the family.
May I remember the blood ties I have with you,
and at least sometimes give my Father
and your Father
pride in what I do. Amen.

Son of Man

Lord Jesus,
you know the joys and pleasures,
the pains and difficulties,
of having an earthly mother and father.
Be with me in my relationships with my parents,
so that these relationships
may be based in your love.
Amen.

God the Holy Spirit

Ruach (Hebrew for spirit, breath, wind)

Breathe life into my dead bones, Spirit of God.*
Stir me with a wind that is strong and true.
Fill the void in my life†
with your power.
Fulfil your promise, and give me hope. Amen.

* Ezekiel 37:1–14 † Genesis 1:2

Spirit of God

Spirit of God, you move where you will,*
and as you will.
To me, your movement is mysterious.
And yet it is planned for my good
and for the good of all.
Spirit of God, help me to bend with
the gentle breeze that you provide. Amen.

* John 3:8

Comforter

Comforter,
allow me to know your comfort,
so that in times of need and distress
I may comfort others. Amen.

Comforter,
fill the empty spaces
that people have in their lives
with your presence and the love of Christ.
Amen.

Counsellor

Why, O Lord, do we so often neglect
the advice and good counsel
of those who would help us?
Make us open to the encouragement
and urgings of others. Amen.

Wonderful Counsellor,
open my mind
and thoughts to your counsel.
Stir me from apathy.
Enliven me with your breath of life,
so that I may know the love of Christ
and live the love of Christ in all I do.
In Jesus' name. Amen.

Worship

Worship is not confined to a church building on Sunday, but these prayers deal with what we call Sunday worship — with preparing for such worship, and with events that take place there.

Before worship

Prepare my heart, Lord;
make me loyal to you;
may I worship you with all my heart. Amen.

Lord God,
be with all those helping today;
may their service give praise to you. Amen.

Lord, open my ears and heart,
and the ears and hearts
of the people gathering here,
to your word and Spirit. Amen.

Guide our worship
this morning/evening, Lord,
so that it may not be just words,
but that we may worship you truly
with our hearts.* Amen.

* Isaiah 29:13

Be with our pastor today, Lord.
May the words he shares
be your word. Amen.

After worship

Allow me, Lord,
to take from this time of worship
your constant love,
to practise justice in my dealings with others,
and to live in humble fellowship with you.*
Amen.

* Micah 6:8

Lord God,
as we hear your blessing,
help us to take all that we have heard and received
into our daily lives. Amen.

Spirit of God, rule our lives.
Fill us with your power.
Give us a generous measure
of joy and hope and peace and love
to share. Amen.

As you have replenished us with love, Jesus,
so let us replenish the lives of those
we meet in this coming week. Amen.

Thank you, God,
for the joyful singing,
for the words of praise,
for the chance to confess my sins,
and again to hear and receive
your wonderful forgiveness,
for the sharing of the prayers,
for your truth penetrating my very being,
for the fellowship of my brothers and sisters in you!
Amen.

Reflections on holy communion

Preparation

Lord God, examine me as only you can.
May the clear light of Jesus
replace the darkness of my sin.
May your death on the cross
bring life into my dying bones.
For the sake of my Lord Jesus Christ,
declare me clean. Amen.

As I look at my life, Lord,
I see so much that disgraces me,
pulls me down, and takes me away from you.
Draw me to you through your living word,
through your loving presence,
through your body and blood. Amen.

Before communion

Lord, I believe; help my unbelief!*
As I come to this table, Lord,
fill me with your truth —
your body and blood
in the bread and wine.
Strengthen me with your presence. Amen.

* Mark 9:24

Sometimes I wonder, Lord,
should I go to communion?
But then I hear your words:
'Take and eat';
'Drink of this, all of you'.
Let me take up your invitation
now and always. Amen.

During holy communion

Lord Jesus,
as I think about those attending communion,
I have to admit that sometimes I wonder:
How can that person go to this meal?
Forgive me for being such a pharisee.
Unite us through your mysterious power.
Make us one as you are one. Amen.

This meal, Lord, reminds us
that you give yourself so freely.
As we receive your love and forgiveness,
free us to give of ourselves. Amen.

After communion

Thank you, Lord Jesus Christ,
for your gift of life and eternity.
Help me to live in you,
today and this week. Amen.

Again today, Lord Jesus,
you've performed a miracle in my life.
As I live in your forgiveness,
help me to see the miracles
you continually make happen. Amen.

It's amazing that again we are one body, Lord.
Separation and division and differences
are healed in your love. Thanks, God.
Keep us one. Remind us that in you
we can overcome our differences,
and work together for the common good.
Amen.

Relating communion to everyday life

We bring bread, Lord,
baked by human hands,
placed in human palms,
eaten by human beings.
Speak your word of life:
This is my body — given for you.

We bring wine, Lord,
made by human endeavour,
tasted by human lips,
swallowed by human throats.
Speak your word of life:
This is my blood — shed for you. Amen.

The gifts we bring are indications
of our fallen, artificial lives:
bread made from wheat
boosted by chemicals;
wine made from grapes
protected by sprays!

Take our imperfect gifts, Lord,
and return them to us restored.
Through your word,
give life, won by Jesus' death,
give love, perfected in your love,
give reality — in your body and blood.
Amen.

Baptism

Often we walk into church and
— zap, there's a baptism
— a family we don't know
— a family we may never see again.
You might like to use the following prayers
concerning that situation.

Before baptism

Lord, if there is a baptism today,
let its power be felt by all!
As your gift of the Holy Spirit
is given to the child,
let the Spirit's power also touch the hearts
of the parents and sponsors, relatives and friends.
Give our pastor power in his preaching,
so that your word may be heard clearly.
Give us power to be friendly,
so that we may make these strangers welcome.
Powerful Holy Spirit, be here today. Amen.

Lord, as I see in my mind these people
who don't know our church and our ways,
I thank you that our pastor is faithful.
Bless the time he has spent in preparation
with this family,
and on this service.
Open their ears and my ears,
their hearts and my heart,
to your word of truth,
and your deeds of love. Amen.

After baptism

The church was filled with strangers, Lord!
Why did I feel so uneasy at their presence?
Replace my unease with love,
as you have replaced this child's sin
with forgiveness. Amen.

Baptism of an older person

We praise you, Lord of mercy,
for the step _____ is taking today.
As the seed of your love is sown,
encourage those of us who know _____
to water that seed well,
so that you may give growth. Amen.

Giver of life,
work in _____'s heart today,
and keep his/her body, soul, and mind
in your care always. Amen.

General

There was a baptism at church today, Lord.
May I remember my baptism.
Thank you, O Father, for the
gift of your Holy Spirit;
for the nurture provided by
parents and teachers,
friends and pastors;
for the love and acceptance
shown by fellow worshippers;
for the forgiveness and eternal life
won by your Son.
Thanks, Lord, for your generosity! Amen.

Thanks, Lord, that another person
was received into your family today.
As members of this family,
help us to respond to the demands and needs
of this spiritual infant,
so that together we may grow in your love,
and as part of your body. Amen.

Daily remembrance

Lord, you make it so easy
through the use of such a common item
as water.

Remind me of when you washed me clean
every time I drink from the tap,
take a shower,
water the garden,
wash my hands,
do the dishes,
enjoy a refreshing swim.

As you allow us to use water
for so many everyday activities,
encourage us to take the blessings
of our baptism
into our everyday life. Amen.

Seasons of the Church Year

Church seasons highlight special events, and help us to focus on the life of Jesus and his body, the church.

Advent

When, Lord, will you come again?
I long for your presence in this world.
I know you are here now —
through your Holy Spirit,
in your word,
in baptism and holy communion,
but I am waiting for the promise to be fulfilled.
Come, Lord Jesus, into this world;
come into my world;
stir me, encourage me,
challenge me,
point my vision forward
to that time when our waiting
will seem but a blink of the eye.
Fill me with excitement, and anticipation,
and preparation as I wait for your coming.
Amen.

Christmas

God, Christmas is at once clear,
and yet a mystery.
Jesus has been born into this world,
bringing peace and bringing division!
Yet I wonder, Lord,
why did you choose this way?
Why not come with angels and in glory?
Help me to realise that glory is
not in the show,
    but in the humility,
not in the casual praise,
    but in the hard work and suffering,
not in the easy way out,
    but in the willingness
to be fully human while fully divine.

At this time, Lord,
I praise you with your great names:
Immanuel,
Prince of Peace,
Everlasting Father,
Wonderful Counsellor.
Teach me to praise you in my living too.
Amen.

Epiphany

Lord Jesus,
help me to take news of you to the world.
Whether my world is international, or suburban;
country town, or local school;
mother's club, or bowling green;
business suits, or casual dress;
help me to identify where and when
I can share the news about you.
Let me realise that sharing may simply be done
in everyday activities —
as I go about my daily tasks
regularly and faithfully.
Guide me to pinpoint opportunities,
and to use them
    to be there,
    to listen,
    to serve,
    to care,
    to assist;
and as I do so,
let your glory be seen in all the world.
Amen.

Lent

Lord, where are you?
Why is life so lonely and bitter?
When I share, I get hurt;
when I hurt, I get bitter;
when I'm bitter,
I don't know where you are, God.

But you are God.
You know where I am.*
Take my bitterness, Lord;
take my hurt;
take my questioning and worry.

And you did, Jesus —
as your shoulders sagged on the cross,
my needs added to your weight.
Thank you, Lord Jesus,
for being so generous,
so available, so able
to walk through the valley yourself,
and suffer loneliness and scorn and hurt,
and experience pain and death.
Lord Jesus, for going there before me,
I thank you. Amen.

* Psalm 139

At the cross

Lord Jesus, I come to this cross,
not to worship the cross itself,
nor the wood it is made from —
other parts of which are used
only for firewood or furniture —
but to focus on your suffering,
    your rejection,
    your death,
and, as shown by the *empty* cross,
your resurrection.
As I bring to you my hurts,
    my tensions,
    my confusions,
    my rejections,
    my sufferings,
    my temptations,
    my hopes,
    my life —
come to me with
    your reassurance,
    your word of forgiveness,
    your reconciliation.
So, restore me to your presence,
to know your compassion,
to feel your love,
to give you praise and honour.
In your name. Amen.

Good Friday

Lord Jesus,
I try to imagine you on the cross —
the suffering, the pain, the humiliation —
and I shudder.
I shudder not only at what you went through,
but at the fact that I was part
of the reason you were there.

I imagine the shouts, the jeering, the insults,
and think: how can they?
But then realise that
I too insult you and jeer at you
by my words and actions.

My imagination has become real —
was real for you;
change me, Lord.
Let me realise that this Friday is good
because you are God. Amen.

Easter

Lord, thank you for signs of Easter:
For the empty tomb,
    which signifies power over death,
    which lets me know dying is not the end,
    which challenges me to ask:
    What am I looking for?*
For the green shoot,
    the symbol of new life,
    which lets me know
    that being alive is important,
    which challenges me to look for
    signs of growth.
For the butterfly
    with its vibrant colours,
    which lets me know of freedom and flight,
    which challenges me to seek
    new adventures and pastures.
For the frog,
    which began its existence
    as a humble tadpole,
    which lets me know
    there is life beyond the murky depths,
    which challenges me to look
    to a changed future.
For life eternal,
    which gives meaning to life now,
    and challenges me to live
    with you. Amen.

* Luke 24:5

Pentecost

Sometimes, Lord,
we call this the birth of the church.
Perhaps rebirth would be a better description.
Whatever it is,
renew me today, Christ, in your image.
Let your Holy Spirit come into my life —
like a strong rushing wind,
which has power and force in it —
to move me and shake me.
Help me to let go
of that which is hindering
my faith in you,
and my relationships with others.
Give me courage to reach out and to take
that tentative step towards a new experience
of walking each day with you,
of talking regularly with you,
of running sometimes
in the direction you show,
even falling and being willing to be picked up
by you again,
of experiencing life in all its fullness*
according to your promise.
I ask these things, Jesus,
knowing the capability of the Holy Spirit
to work with dead bones†
and to work in me. Amen.

* John 10:10 † Ezekiel 37:1–14

Fruits of the Spirit

Galatians chapter 5 lists nine fruits of the Spirit. They are not easy to exercise, but God has given them to us for our use, and for the good of the community.

Love

Thanks, Lord, for love,
for love shown in all kinds of ways:
Love from a friend,
when providing support in times of need.
Love from a child,
who loves me as a parent
even when I don't deserve it.
Love from colleagues,
who speak encouraging and challenging words.
Love from a pet,
who gives a greeting of unbridled joy
each time I walk in the gate. Amen.

Thanks, Lord,
for creating so many kinds of love:
Love from a parent,
even when that love is in the form of 'no'!
Love from a teacher,
who puts in that extra effort for me.
Love from a spouse,
who has the courage to point out failings.
Love from those from whom I expect no love,
but who reach out and touch by their actions.
Thanks, Lord, for love.
Most of all, Lord Jesus Christ,
thanks for your love,
a lasting, patient, undeserved love
given freely and often.
Help me to live in that love. Amen.

Joy

Joy to the world! Help me to join in the chorus
and sing to you, Lord.

Sometimes joy is elusive,
because joy is distinct
from laughter and gaiety,
from frivolity and fun.
They all help to make me happy,
but joy is somehow different.

Lord, were you joyful
when people responded
to your touch, your word?
Was there sadness present at the attitudes
of those who mocked and rejected and plotted?
Perhaps joy is tinged with sadness.

Jesus, I feel joy deep down in my bones —
but it's not something that's
going to bubble over.
Rather, it's a reassuring presence,
a strength in time of danger,
a calm in the clamour of life,
a support when things collapse around me.
God of joy, fill me with your joy.
Let me join with heaven and nature,
with people and beasts,
to share your joy with the world. Amen.

Peace (1)

Lord Jesus, what is peace?

I read the daily newspapers —
there's no peace there.
I watch the TV news and current affairs —
there's no peace there.
Even on the soapies —
cheating, hurt, bitterness,
scandal, but no peace.

Lord Jesus, what is peace?

When I consider the farmers
battling to save the farm,
is there peace?
When I look at last year's year 12s
repeating or searching for work,
is there peace?
When I see families torn apart
by violence and selfishness,
is there peace?

Lord Jesus, what is peace?

'Peace is what I leave with you; it is my own peace that I give you. I do not give it as the world does.'*

Lord Jesus, what is peace? Amen.

* John 14:27 TEV

Peace (2)

Lord Jesus, give me your peace.

Give me confidence in the depths of danger.
Give me hope when I am surrounded by fear.
Still my worries, calm the anxieties
pressing in on me from the world I live in.

Lord Jesus, give me peace.

Reassure me that you are with me
when I seem to be alone.
Ease my doubting, as you did Thomas's.*

Lord Jesus, give me peace.

Guide my searching for peace,
so that I may not seek it
where it is not to be found,
but that I may seek it in you.

Lord Jesus, live in me
and give me your peace. Amen.

* John 20:27,28

Patience

I know a bit about patience, Lord —
or at least impatience!

Waiting for those who are late annoys me!
Fixing up people's mistakes frustrates me!
Sitting at traffic lights is the pits!

Forgive me, Lord,
for missing the opportunities:
the opportunities to listen to those
who want to talk for a few precious moments;
the opportunities to be creative
and encourage folk to stretch themselves;
the opportunities to reflect and pray.

Make me aware that the little times
I consider so important
are but a pinpoint in your sight.
And so help me not to waste these occasions,
but to make them useful to me,
and to those around me.
In your name, and in your time. Amen.

Kindness

Lord Jesus, help me to be kind:

to keep my mouth shut so I do not hurt;
to close my eyes to those events
to which I react angrily;
to allow my ears the luxury
of not hearing words that make me bite;
to help me not only turn the other cheek,
but to let my whole body accept bruises
in your name;
to control my nose
so that the aromas it experiences
are incense in your sight.

Lord Jesus, help me to be kind. Amen.

Goodness

Lord God, it's not really cool to be good!
Does that mean we should be bad?
Help me to distinguish between good and bad,
to hand the bad in my life over to you
to deal with,
to take time to develop and nurture the good.

I remember, Creator God, you said: It is good.*
Help me to reclaim your goodness
in all of creation;
to take what is good in your sight,
and make it a blessing —
goodness for all around me.

Thanks, Lord, for your goodness
and kindness and patience. Amen.

* Genesis 1

Goodness gracious!
Yes, Lord,
your grace is something to be marvelled at,
and your goodness is seen everywhere.
Help us to thank you
for your goodness and graciousness,
and not waste words unnecessarily. Amen.

Faithfulness

Faithful God,
forgive me when I am unfaithful
to you in my actions,
and in my words;
to my spouse in my thoughts,
and when I don't support her/him
in front of the children;
to my children
when I criticise unfairly,
or tease them in front of their friends. Amen.

Faithful God,
teach me faithfulness.
As you are faithful to me,
so let my life proclaim you.
As you have loved me,
so challenge me to love my spouse
according to your precepts.*
As you support and accept me as your child,
so help me to accept my children,
and build them up through praise. Amen.

* Ephesians 5:21–33

Humility

Lord Jesus, make me humble,
as you were humble. Amen.

Help me, Lord, in all I do, to be self-effacing;
to accept praise with graciousness;
to use what I have been given
for the benefit of all;
to creatively lower my standard of living,
so that others may live. Amen.

Obedient Jesus, teach me obedience.
Help me to learn humility as a gift from God,
and a gift to my neighbour. Amen.

Self-control

Lord God, Creator — we thank you
for bringing order into this chaotic world.*

Through your Son, Jesus,
bring self-control into my disordered life.
Replace the chaos of sin and rejection
with the self-control of love and acceptance.

Let your Holy Spirit so guide my life
that what is out of control and reckless
may become controlled and caring,
useful and restrained.

We pray under your controlling influence.
Amen.

* Genesis 1:2

Church life

Church life is varied and interesting. There is something for everyone to do. These prayers thank God for all those who help in their various ways.

Administration

Lord Jesus,
guide those people in our congregation
who have taken on the responsibility
of administration.
Give them wisdom, patience, and humour
as they deal with both challenging
and mundane issues.
Allow them to see
that excellence in administration
assists and allows
for your good news to be proclaimed. Amen.

Be with the state and national leaders
of our church, Lord.
They work under much pressure and stress.
Encourage me to support them through prayer,
and words and letters of appreciation.
When they face difficult decisions,
give them wisdom.
When hard choices are to be made,
give them strength.
When they see results from your word,
give them joy. Amen.

Fellowship

Thanks, Lord Jesus, for calling me
into fellowship with you,
and with my fellow worshippers and believers.
Help us to see that our fellowship
goes much deeper than our desires,
but is rooted in your love.
Draw us together through your word,
through the breaking of bread,
through worship,
through praise,
and through the community you create.
Amen.

Nurture

Lord Jesus, you spent time learning
at your father's side in the carpenter's shop,
and in your Father's house from the Scriptures.
Help me to take the opportunities to learn
from your life and example
as spelt out in the Bible,
from my pastor and leaders
in our congregation.
Be with those who are given
the tasks of nurturing,
so that they may be faithful to your word,
and helpful in my life. Amen.

Service

Lord, I am often reminded that you came
'not to be served, but to serve',*
and yet I find it so hard to be a servant.
Certainly there have been many times
when I could have taken part
in an act of service,
but shied away. Forgive me, Lord.
Challenge me to respond
to the needs and events
where I can be of service,
and so serve others as you served me. Amen.

* Mark 10:45; Matthew 20:28

Witness

'But I can't witness, Lord; I have no training!'
Help me to see that the only training I need
I received in my baptism!

Help me to see that witnessing is not only
going out to convert the world,
but that I can be a witness to your love
in my everyday life.
Allow me to live so close to you
that your love shines through all I do,
and I learn to be a witness
without even realising that I'm doing it! Amen.

Worship

Dear Lord,
it was a habit of yours to worship regularly.
Move in our hearts
that we may worship you regularly. Amen.

So many, Lord,
are involved in planning and running worship.
Guide each person who contributes,
in whatever way.
Be with the pastor in his proclaiming.
Be with the musicians and singers
as they praise you.
Be with the ushers and welcomers,
the stewards and readers,
those who prepare morning tea,
and greet their fellow worshippers with a smile;
those who prepare floral arrangements
or make banners that tell of your love.
Be with those who operate the sound system,
and the ones whose work
is not done in full view,
but is appreciated by everyone — the cleaners.
And may I worship you, Lord,
whatever my role may be. Amen.

For councils and boards

Lord, we are here. Send us!*
But first, cleanse us and renew us.
Allow us to live in your image!

Guide us as the elected council/board of _____,
so that we may be your servants,
and lead where you would have us lead,
and go where you would have us go.

In Jesus' name we pray. Amen.

* Isaiah 6:5–8

Committees

Lord, allow the committees
of our congregation
not to get bogged down
with endless discussion,
but to be places of intellectual stimulation,
and hives of activity,
so that your will is done,
and your name is glorified. Amen.

Women's fellowship

I don't know, Lord,
whether the women's group
is the backbone of our congregation or not.
But I do know that their contribution
to the life of our community is enormous.
Bless and guide them

that they may be encouraged
in their activities.
Lord, we appreciate their work as Marthas;
motivate them to spend time as Marys too. Amen.

Sunday school

May our Sunday school be a place
where your word is proclaimed,
and your love is shared,
so that all who attend
may hear your truth,
and live in you, Jesus. Amen.

Kid's club

Some people say it's too noisy;
some don't know how we manage
with so many kids;
some wonder about the value and worth
of children meeting on a week night;
but you, Lord, have given your promise to be
where two or three, or 33 or 143,
are gathered in your name.*
We've grabbed hold of your promise, Lord,
and we believe it.
Give strength, ability, and patience
to the leaders and organisers
of our children's club,
so that all may share the gospel,
and your name may be praised. Amen.

* Matthew 18:20

Musicians

I thank you, Lord, for those who
freely use the ability you have given them
to lead our worship with music:
for the organist,
who lifts our singing to new heights;
for the choir conductor, who is meticulous,
so that the choir's offering
may be a gift to you;
for the band,
who are willing to give different people a go
and teach us new songs
with which we can praise you;
for the time all of these put into their practice,
so that our worship
may be of an excellent standard,
and give praise to you. Amen.

Cleaners

Lord, they're often not seen,
but their work is seen.
Thanks, God, that some of our folk
are willing to do the menial tasks of
dusting, sweeping, vacuuming.
Help me to see that
when work I consider to be menial
is done to praise you,
it is as important as anything else.
Thanks, God, for the cleaners. Amen.

Church structure

Lord Jesus, your attitude to structures
seemed to be two-fold.
You had no time for those
that promoted self-interest,
exploited human wants,
and were inappropriate;
but you worked with human organisations,
within structures where needs were met.
Guide us that we may distinguish between
self-interested and inappropriate structures,
and those that will help and encourage us
to meet the needs of others,
and promote your kingdom. Amen.

Ushers

For good order and decorum,
I give you praise, Lord Jesus.

I thank you for those who act as ushers
in our congregation,
who sacrifice their worship time
so that I may know where to sit
and when to go forward to communion,
who provide service orders and bulletins,
who keep a record
of how many attend church.

Lord, protect them
so they do not get too caught up
in their busyness and lose sight of you. Amen.

Welcomers

The different styles of welcomers
intrigue me, Lord.
Some thrust out their hand to shake,
others greet me loudly,
while still others are timid
and politely say Welcome.
But all of them smile at me,
and all of them make me and others
feel welcome.
May we have the same joy
in our worship and lives
as there is in the smile of welcome.
Amen.

Floral decorations

I don't always understand
what the flowers are saying, Lord;
but I do know that they help me praise you.
The bright reds and yellows
remind me of your radiance.
The sombre greys and silvers
talk to me of your suffering and compassion.
I praise you, God,
for the creative ability used by those
who decorate your house
with flowers and greenery. Amen.

Banners

O Lord, there are so many ways to praise you.
I get pleasure out of the banners
in our church —
and I hope you do too.
The different banners with each church season
help me to think through
the various emphases.
The different messages challenge me,
and add to the depth of my worship time.
Thanks, Lord Jesus, for the gifts and thoughts
shared by the talented banner makers. Amen.

SECTION 2

Daily work and business

To use our hands, to be intellectually stimulated, to help someone, to use our time wisely — all these are aspects of the wider daily task of working for a living. Let's use the abilities God has given us.

Thanks for work

Thanks, Lord,
for the opportunity to do things I enjoy,
and to get paid for it.

May I use the wages I receive
in a way that recognises that both
my ability to work and
my reward for this work,
first of all, comes from you. Amen.

Pride in work

Lord, in a time when lots of people
are struggling to find satisfaction
in their daily work,
make me grateful for a job,
make me grateful for workmates
to share ideas with.

Make me grateful for the challenge
of using my abilities
to match the demands
of the position I am in. Amen.

For those out of work

So many people are out of work, Lord.
Forgive me when I accuse them
of being 'bludgers'.
Even if I can't understand their feelings,
allow me to be sympathetic to their plight.
As you befriended the homeless
and the helpless, Jesus,
encourage me to befriend the workless
and those struggling for identity. Amen.

Ethics in business

Lord, it's so easy to cheat;
not so much to lie,
as not to tell the truth.

Give those who are faced with difficult choices
the courage and ability to choose,
not that which will result in the most profit,
or in the easy promotion,
but that which is honest and
in keeping with their faith in you, and
fair and just in their dealings
with their fellow workers. Amen.

For those forced off the land

A loss brings grieving, Lord;
the loss of land, or of a job,
the loss of a loved one, or of an old friend.

Lord, I pray that you would be with those
who have lost,
or look as if they'll lose, their land —
perhaps a farm that's been in the family
for so long no-one remembers;
perhaps a recent acquisition,
which looked so promising,
but which has turned sour through
high interest rates and bad seasons.
Whatever the case, the sense of loss, the grief,
the disappointment, the tension, remains.

God, comfort them
as a God who knows what loss is —
as a God who saw his people lose their land
through their following of other gods;
as a God who lost his own Son,
so that the lost might be found;
as a God who still experiences loss
every time someone turns their back on you.

God, as you know the need of comfort,
provide your comfort. Amen.

Lord of the land,
be with those who are facing the loss
of their land.

Allow them to give thanks to you
for the privilege
of being your steward on that block
for so many years.

Give them the insight to look forward
to that which you have in store for them to do
in the days and years to come. Amen.

Honesty and justice

What is truth, Lord God?*
Let all those who have work know your truth,
and in response to that truth,
do an honest day's toil,
and give praise to you,
simply by the work of their hands
or their minds.

Allow each of us, in whatever we do,
to practise justice,
to make fairness our trademark,
to recognise the rights of each individual,
and to uphold the dignity
of all those we work under, or serve.
In Jesus' name. Amen.

* John 18:38

Varieties of occupation

Lord Jesus, you knew the joy
of working with wood as a carpenter.
You mixed with tax collectors,
and fishermen, and homemakers,
with teachers of the law,
religious leaders, and physicians.

Thanks, God,
for the variety of occupations that exist.
Allow each of us who has a job
to thank you by using the skills and abilities
you have given us
in the occupation we are in,
so that we may do our best,
fulfil the expectations of our superiors,
provide service of a high quality,
and take pride
in what you have given us to do.

Encourage us always to see our work in context,
as important to you —
because it is a gift from you —
no matter how it may rank in society's eyes.
And allow us, through our work,
to give glory to you,
and to serve our fellow human beings. Amen.

Looking for work

Be with those, Lord God,
who have just finished school
or completed their studies,
and are searching for that right job.

Fill them with enthusiasm and excitement
at the possibilities that exist in their lives.
Give them patience when that longed-for job
is offered to someone else.
Let them see that they still have esteem
in your eyes,
particularly when they have not obtained a job
after a lot of searching.

Make them willing to try their hand at
something different, if that is necessary.
Encourage their creativity in the work
that is at hand.
Help them to build positive relationships
with their new workmates.

May we be compassionate in our support
as their lives change dramatically,
when their hopes are met,
and when their hopes are dashed. Amen.

Travel

Jesus, you spent many hours
walking the dusty roads of Palestine,
as you carried out the work
your Father had given you.

Keep safe all those who spend time
travelling to their job and home again,
driving to meet appointments,
on public transport
in the course of their day's work.

Thanks, Lord Jesus,
for the ease of moving around today.
Help us to use our time travelling wisely.
Amen.

Education

'The getting of wisdom' is a major pursuit today. Thank God for the wide variety of learning opportunities.

General

Lord Jesus, help us to be true disciples,
willing to learn, willing to experience,
willing to experiment, willing to change,
knowing our foundation is in you,
the changeless Christ. Amen.

For teachers

Lord, you were addressed as Teacher,
and felt the pressures of giving right answers
and providing correct information.
Be with all those
who have the call to be a teacher.
Give them knowledge in their chosen subjects,
confidence as they face difficult situations,
enthusiasm to share information
with the students,
a willingness to support the slow learners,
and joy when their pupils
take pleasure in learning;
in your name, Teacher and Lord. Amen.

For students

I pray, Lord, that you would be with
children and teenagers,
as they progress
through their various stages of schooling.
Help them to realise the value
of what they are learning.
Give them a cooperative and enthusiastic spirit.
Allow them to cherish
the friendships they form,
and to learn, not only academic school work,
but also the worth of relationships. Amen.

May the students of our schools, O Lord,
receive a well-rounded education,
through which they learn to think creatively
and find mental stimulation;
to relate socially
and form friendships of lasting value;
to enjoy physical exercise,
and win or lose graciously;
to participate in various activities,
and contribute to the growth
of those around them.
Allow them in years to come to look back
and see their school days as time well spent.
In your name. Amen.

Junior primary schools

I thank you, Lord, for those teachers
who are willing to work with young children.
As they mould their developing minds,
let them do so creatively,
with responsibility and enthusiasm
so that the students
are continually encouraged
in their pursuit of learning. Amen.

Senior primary schools

Lord, be with the children
in the senior years of primary school.
May they appreciate the wider challenges
that they are faced with.
As they learn to interact socially,
and attend camps and interschool sports,
allow them to remember
those events are part of their education,
and participate willingly.
Give the teachers life and fervour;
a passion to teach and share;
concern for relationships;
and a warmth in all their dealings
with the children in their care. Amen.

High school students

Lord,
as students mature,
physically and emotionally,
as they rebel and challenge,
as they consider and make decisions,
as they learn interesting facts
and as they wonder about the point
of some subjects,
open their minds to learning,
open their hearts to compassion,
give them the freedom
to express their emotions,
and enable them to cope
with their bodily changes,
so that they may grow into mature,
committed,
intelligent,
passionate young adults. Amen.

High school teachers

Lord Jesus,
may the teachers of my children
know the joy of sharing,
the challenge of teaching,
the rigour of discipline.
May they respond positively to the pressures
that come upon them,
and look forward to each day and each lesson
with renewed vigour and enthusiasm. Amen.

Tertiary

For schools of higher discipline
and academic pursuit,
I give you praise, O Lord. Amen.

Universities

Thanks, Lord, for places of higher learning.
Be with those who are studying at universities,
so that they may be challenged
in their thinking,
prompted to explore new ideas,
and bold enough to stand up for
what they believe in.

Give those involved in research
and experimentation
respect for what they are working with,
and courage and dignity in their dealings
with their fellow human beings
and with the created world. Amen.

Lord of the universe,
bless the universities of the world. Amen.

Other tertiary institutions

God, creator of all, and sharer of knowledge,
there are so many different things to study,
so much to learn and discover.
Thank you for the variety of subject choices,
the diversity of learning institutions.
May all those studying,
experimenting, discovering,
learning, growing,
do so to the best of their ability,
so that when they graduate
they may be able to serve humankind,
and give praise to you,
through their talents and gifts. Amen.

Education for workers

Lord, I have taken advantage of courses
provided for workers.
It's a good feeling to broaden our horizons.
Thanks, Lord, for the distinct character
of each course and each subject.
Thanks for the lecturers who give of their
time and knowledge so freely.
Thanks for the people
I have met and shared with.
Enable me to use my new-found knowledge
for the benefit of those I deal with every day.
Amen.

Life experiences

Lord Jesus,
give me the ability to learn
from all the experiences my life brings.
Make me open to the prompting
of your Holy Spirit.
Help me to look positively at those things
that challenge, and even disturb me.
Lord, there are so many opportunities to learn;
allow me to value each one. Amen.

In the home

Every morning, every afternoon,
every evening, Lord,
situations occur in our home
which allow for one or more of the family
to learn something.
May we not be scared to admit
we were wrong, Lord.
May we be open to the different possibilities
that exist in each activity.
Take away our stubbornness.
Replace it with conviction and openness.
May we be grateful for those who are willing to
help us learn and better ourselves.
Thanks, Lord, for learning opportunities.
Amen.

Communication

Communication

I thank you, Lord,
for a tongue to speak
and ears to listen.
Give me discernment, so that I may know
when to speak and when to be silent,
when to listen and when to pay attention.
Amen.

Thanks, God of communication,
for modern means of communication;
may I take control of them,
and not let them control me. Amen.

Letters

Lord, I like receiving letters;
sometimes my friends delight me
with their news;
sometimes I shed tears
at the emotions they express.
Thanks, Lord, that I can read
and write.
May I write letters that stimulate,
and share, and build up relationships.
Amen.

Writing letters

Lord Jesus,
allow me to use my gift of letter-writing
    to encourage,
    to challenge,
    to bring good news,
    to sympathise when bad news is received,
    to express thanks for effort put in,
    to give support when support is needed.
Amen.

Thanks, Lord, for the mail service,
which allows me to keep in touch via letters
with my friends and relatives. Amen.

Talking

Thanks, God,
that I can talk with my family and friends.
Help me to use this gift
    to build up and encourage,
    to challenge and correct in love,
    to support and praise.
Allow my speech to reflect your love.
In Jesus' name. Amen.

Teach me, Lord, to communicate more,
and talk less. Amen.

Telephone

The telephone is ringing again, Lord.
So often!
Tonight I wish the telephone wasn't invented!

But I can remember the time it rang,
and my friend spoke with me for a long time
about family and work,
and health and relationships.
That day, Lord, I appreciated the telephone!

Thanks, God, that you allow men and women
skills and wisdom to develop such a convenient
network of communication
structured around the telephone.
Help me to use it in such a way that others
may appreciate it too.
Thank you that it's so easy to reach the person
I wish to talk to.

Remind me, Lord,
that you are as close as the telephone,
and in fact even closer. Amen.

Television

It educates, it mesmerises;
it provides company,
it dominates relationships.

Lord, at times television has a powerful impact
on our lives —
too powerful.
Allow me to control it,
and not the other way around.

Thank you for those shows
that entertain and educate,
that interest and inform.
Give me the self-esteem and control
to switch off
the programs that manipulate and degrade.
Help all people to use their TV sets in a manner
that is fitting,
and in a way that does not damage
their relationships
or downgrade the reputations of
their fellow human beings.

Thanks, Lord,
for the numerous occupations that are
provided in this medium.
May each worker be filled
with a sense of service,
and through their role give praise to you.
Amen.

Radio (1)

Thanks for the companionship
of my radio, Lord:
to share in the talkback;
to be informed by the interesting guests;
to relax to my favourite music;
to be up-to-date
in the world of sports and politics.
All these occur because of the miracle of radio.
Thanks, Lord. Amen.

Radio (2)

As I push the button on the car radio
or twist the dial at home,
the amazing smorgasbord
of sounds and programs astounds me.
Thanks, Lord,
for the variety of music and personalities,
for the different programs and angles,
that are presented each day on different stations.
Amen.

Radio (3)

God,
may I be tolerant
of what other people wish to hear;
may I be discerning in what I listen to;
may the programs and presenters
have good taste in their choices;
may the gift of radio
reflect your gift of communication. Amen.

For Christian radio stations

It seems that more and more
Christian radio stations
are up and running in our land.
Guide them, Lord of communication,
that their goals and aims
may reflect your purposes.
Give them enthusiasm, prayer,
and financial support,
so that they may not only witness
through your word,
but also through their professionalism
and excellence.
I pray in the name of the great communicator,
Jesus of Nazareth. Amen.

The local paper

Thanks, Jesus, that we are able to keep up with
the news of the local community —
to share in their successes
and joyful times;
to commiserate with their losses
and their times of anxiety.
Help us to use these local tidbits of news
as stepping stones to support and love others,
as opportunities to help and encourage.
As we read about our neighbours
in the words of the local newspaper,
may we bring your word to them
through our presence and actions. Amen.

The daily paper
(state-wide or national newspaper)

Thanks, Lord, for those who daily
bring us information on
sport and business,
tragedies and joys,
the wider community and international events,
government, and human-interest stories.
Fill the journalists and editors with
a sense of responsibility,
so that their reporting may be
worthwhile and interesting,
and may serve the purpose
of keeping people informed and aware.
Help them and us to avoid
the scandalous, the rumour,
the ill-informed, the misreported.
Forgive them and us for any failures.
Challenge them and us to be worthy servants
of you and of each other. Amen.

On computers

Help me to remember, Lord,
that the computer you have placed in my skull
is so much more creative
and intelligent and powerful
than the computer sitting on my desk. Amen.

Thank you, Lord,
for the advances of modern science.
I'm amazed at what my computer can do.
Often, I'm also mystified
at how to get it to do it.
Give me patience and wisdom
in my use of the computer. Amen.

Be with those who invent
and design and instruct —
that their inventions
may be for the common good;
that their designs may take advantage
of the latest technology;
that their instruction may be kept simple
and be useful to many people. Amen.

Thank you, Lord,
for giving me the abilities and opportunities
to develop keyboard skills.
May I use them
    to serve,
    to challenge,
    to prod,
    to facilitate,
    to share the good things
you have shared with me. Amen.

Final prayer

May these ways of communication
be used to your glory, Lord Jesus.
Amen.

Transport

We have such a variety of transport. As you use your particular daily means of transport, why not give thanks to God for it?

Bikes

Thanks, Lord,
for touring bikes, and mountain bikes,
for tandems and three-wheelers.

Thanks for the fun we can have as a family,
when out on a ride together.

Thanks, God,
for councils and other interested groups,
who provide safe and interesting bike tracks.
Amen.

Lord, keep safe those who ride bicycles.
Give them sense,
and respect for other road-users.
Make drivers of cars and other vehicles alert
to the presence of bikes on busy roads.
Let all vehicles be used
in a safe and worthwhile manner. Amen.

Planes

Watching a plane take off seems to fascinate
so many people, Lord of miracles.
And it is a miracle that such a heavyweight
can lift effortlessly into the air.
Help us to see the everyday miracles you
provide in our lives, Lord. Amen.

Thanks, Lord, for the miracle of flight,
for the ease of getting
from one place to another.

Thanks, Lord, for the training given to pilots,
for the skill they exhibit each time they fly.

Thanks, Lord, for stewards,
who make our journeys more comfortable,
who serve us with refreshments.

Thanks, Lord, for ground staff,
who handle our luggage,
who wish us well after a long flight.

Thanks, Lord, for taxis,
and relatives and friends,
who drop us off,
and pick us up at airports.

Thanks, Lord, for motivating all these people.
Amen.

Cars

Is the bumper-to-bumper peak-hour traffic
worth it, Lord?
Does the pollution caused by excessive braking
and accelerating give you pleasure, God?
Is our selfish dependence on the use of a car
in keeping with your desire
for us to care for each other?

Let us use the opportunities that arise
when we need to travel across town
to give support to a friend in need;
to help our aged relatives with their shopping,
or doctor's appointment;
to offer a lift to our children and their friends;
to carry goods for our friends
who are shifting home.

Thanks, Lord,
for those who have the ability to design
and produce the cars.
Give us the ability to use it wisely. Amen.

Bus

So often, Lord Jesus,
I see a bus go by half empty!
Is it because of our need
to get somewhere in a hurry
or the inconvenience caused
by not having door-to-door service?

Lord, teach us to use the services provided,
to use the time available for reading or praying,
to appreciate the way we can do a little for the
environment — your creation —
by taking a bus instead of the car. Amen.

Walking

Walking is becoming popular again, Lord.
It was popular in your day too!
Thanks, God, that so many have rediscovered
the joy and benefit of walking —
whether a stroll in the park,
a brisk early-morning starter,
the exercise of a power-walk,
or relaxing with friends.

Thanks, God, for legs and energy
to enjoy this gift you have given us. Amen.

Four-wheel drive vehicles

For the thrill of off-road driving,
for being able to go to places
that are not accessible in normal vehicles,

for the opportunity of getting away from it all:
I thank you, Lord.

Lord, be with all those who own
a 4WD vehicle —
that they may be sensible in their driving,
that they may be kept safe in their adventures,
that they may respect
the properties they drive through,
and through their experiences
of nature and your creation,
that they may see you and grow close to you.

Lord of creation, and Lord of our lives,
I pray this in Jesus' name. Amen.

Motorbikes

Lord God,
sometimes I shudder when I see the risks
motorbike riders take.
Keep them safe, Lord.
Keep them sensible in their riding habits.
Give them wisdom to use the power and agility
of their bikes for a worthwhile purpose.

Keep alert those driving in cars,
so they may appreciate the power of bikes
and not cause situations where
accidents and injury may occur.
Help all users of the road to respect each other
and to encourage each other to travel safely.
Amen.

Semitrailers/trucks

Thanks, God,
for the power of reticulated vehicles.
As these monsters of the road travel our nation,
give their drivers stamina,
keep them alert,
give them patience when pushed for time.
Allow them to enjoy the companionship
offered by the roadhouses and other truckies.

Lord, be with the families of these drivers,
often left behind,
lonely, waiting, wondering.
Keep them faithful.
Give them joy and happiness when their
spouse and provider returns.
Let them value their time together,
and share fond memories in their times apart.
Amen.

Ships

I am amazed, Lord, by ocean liners.
They are like floating towns on the water.

And seeing the aircraft carrier
floating into the harbour,
with its load of planes and sailors,
I'm amazed at the detail and intricacy
that keeps it working!

And the oil-tanker, with its important load,
seems like a floating giant on the horizon;
I'm amazed at our dependence on this cargo!

Lord of the seas, protect those travelling
in these gigantic ships;
be with those transporting cargo —
large and small, significant and insignificant.

Thanks, Lord, for the genius and creativity
you allow us to use and share. Amen.

Trains

The peak-hour express is running late again —
and it's annoying.

Lord, turn my thoughts from myself.
Help me to think of the driver of this train,
and the pressures he's under.
Give him confidence in his training and ability
to take this rolling monster
safely to its journey's end.
Be with those responsible
for monitoring the tracks,
and adjusting schedules so that all may fit in.

Thanks, Lord, for this service that provides
for me and for so many others
a convenient way of travelling
to and from work. Amen.

Thanks, Lord, for the joy of a ride
on the old-fashioned steam train;
for the chance to escape the humdrum
of everyday life,
and relax in the comfort of the carriages;
for the fuel which gives the engine its power,
and the strength to chug up those steep hills;
for the exhilaration shared
by all the passengers,
as the fresh air billows in the windows;
for those folk
who give of their time and energy
to provide an opportunity
to experience a bygone era.

Help us, Lord, to preserve those good gifts
you allow us to discover. Amen.

Mental health

In this high-tension world, it's important that we not only deal with any problem physically and emotionally, but also that we go to the source of peace, God, in prayer.

Relaxation

Thanks, Lord, for days off,
for moments to myself,
and time to share with my family.
Help me always to set aside time
to relax
and recuperate
and be refreshed.
Lord, I think of those who are so busy,
or so pressured,
that they keep on going,
with little regard to their own health,
or the damage being done to their family.
Let them remember, God, that you rested.*
Let them remember, Jesus, that you took time
to be by yourself.†
Give them the courage to say no,
give them the wisdom to relax,
give them the opportunity
to build up their relationships,
and allow them to return to their duties
refreshed and revitalised. Amen.

* Genesis 2:2,3 † Mark 6:45,46

Criticism

Lord, it's so easy to criticise,
rather than to praise.
Help me to think before I speak.
Open my eyes so that I see the positive actions
of those around me,
instead of the negative ones.
Out of my mouth, God,
allow words of praise and support to come.
Amen.

Lord, I have experienced criticism.
Sometimes it's fair, sometimes it's not.

When there is positive criticism,
allow me to react to it honestly,
to learn from what is said,
to put into practice what is suggested.
Thanks, Lord, for those who have the courage
to confront me in love.

When there is negative criticism,
give me the ability to avoid reacting
in a like manner.
Give me the courage to correct where necessary.
Allow those who are hurting me
with their words
to see the hurt they are causing,
and to retract the phrases that cause pain.

Lord, you experienced criticism,
and you took it to the cross with you.
Take the cross of criticism
I sometimes have to bear,
and make my burden light.* Amen.

* Matthew 11:28–30

Pressure

Deadlines to meet!
Unreal expectations!
Demands from this direction
and that direction!

Lord, as the pressure mounts,
draw me closer to you.
Reassure me of your presence,
of the ability you have given me to cope,
of the need to say no sometimes.
Give me a clear mind
to deal with each item one by one,
and in a way that does justice
to the task at hand.

Lord, as you handled pressure,
so give me the ability
to handle pressure in my life. Amen.

Anger

Lord, I get angry sometimes,
and at other times I get very angry.
Some people say that's wrong,
while others say it's OK.

I remember, Lord, that you became angry —
very angry.*
But it seems that your anger was filled with
zeal for your Father, and with compassion.

Teach me, Lord,
the difference between righteous anger,
which arises out of zeal for you,
and selfish anger, which serves only me.

Teach me to use the one wisely,
and to control the other. Amen.

* Mark 11:15–17; Matthew 23:13–28

Read Psalm 137:7–9

Lord, the writer of this psalm was angry,
and had terrible thoughts.
But he took his anger to you,
and let you deal with it.

Thanks, God, for
taking my anger on yourself.

When I become angry,
when I experience terrible thoughts,
allow me to bring them to you,
and to hand them over to you to deal with. Amen.

Support

Thanks, God, for those
    who lend a listening ear,
    who offer words of advice,
    who steer me in the right direction,
    who let me see you in them. Amen.

Emotion

Jesus, it helps me to know you wept,*
you were tired, you became angry.†
Help me, Lord, to recognise my emotions,
and not to deny them.
Enable me not to be upset by my emotions,
but to see their expression as valuable
for letting off steam,
for relaxing,
for showing how I feel.

At the same time, Lord Jesus, while I ask you to
help me to be free to express my emotions,
assist me to control them,
so that I don't attempt to manipulate
others through my feelings. Amen.

* John 11:35 † John 4:6; 2:13–17

Lord Jesus,
give me the freedom to weep
    as you wept;
  the ability to have compassion,
    as you were compassionate;
  the openness to express sadness
    as you did when saddened;
  the reasons to celebrate,
    as you celebrated with family and friends.
Amen.

Tiredness

When I am weary, God of rest,
give me the ability to learn from you.
As Jesus went away by himself,
help me to make time for myself.
As Jesus relaxed with friends,
so allow me times of relaxation.
As Jesus was strengthened
through his conversation with you,
encourage me to bring my weariness to you.

God of refreshment,
refresh me in my tired times. Amen.

Stress

Lord God, Creator of all things,
Redeemer of the world,
be with those who suffer from stress.
Help them to distinguish
between good stress and bad stress,
between the stress that urges them
to a higher plane,
and the stress that pushes them over the brink.

God, you must know what stress
and pressure are all about.
Free us
so that all stress and pressure in our lives
may work for your glory and our good. Amen.

Busyness

Lord, help me to keep busy!
In whatever I am doing,
let me be active in a way
that is pleasing to you.

Jesus, in my busyness,
help me make time
for those who need my time,
to offer a listening ear
to those who need to talk,
to be present
when my presence can be a comfort.

Lord God, Creator,
you made time for me.
Teach me to make time for others. Amen.

God, you know what it is to be busy,
and to be still;
help me to be still in the midst of a busy life.
Amen.

Depression

God of all comfort,
be with those who suffer from depression.

Relieve their anxieties
by the power of your word
and the presence of your Spirit.
Guide those who work with the depressed,
so that their advice and counsel
may be uplifting and encouraging.

God of all comfort,
comfort the depressed with your comfort.*
Amen.

* Isaiah 40

SECTION 3

Stages of life

In a sense, life is made up of memories and expectations. It's important to remember what we were like at earlier ages, and valuable to appreciate those who have already been at stages we have yet to reach. Thank God for different stages of life.

Birth

Lord, I thank you for this miracle of creation;
for the tiny fingers so perfectly formed;
for the kicking toes and lively legs;
for the eyes —
so small but strong in their looking;
for the crop of hair, amazing in one so young,
but which reminds me of your promise
of care and protection;*
for life — full and fresh and new.

Lord, thanks for allowing me
to take part in your work of creation. Amen.

* Matthew 10:30,31

Lord, thanks for this child
you have given to us,
for the privilege and the responsibility!
Help us to enjoy the privilege —
to share our knowledge and love,
to exercise freedom and caring
as we raise this child.
Keep us mindful of our responsibility —

the need to discipline in love,
to instil respect for all that you have created.

Let the life of this child
bring honour and glory to you. Amen.

Thanks, Lord of life, for babies who bring joy
into the hearts of parents. Amen.

Excitement

Lord Jesus,
the excitement on the children's faces
brings me joy.
May the exciting times in our lives
bring you joy, Lord. Amen.

Children

Lord God,
you provide energy
through so many different sources.
At times,
our children seem to tap into all of them.
Help them to use their energy wisely,
and in a creative way.
Give us patience
when the noise and activity level is high.
And thanks for the quiet periods,
which allow us to reflect and recuperate.
Amen.

Brotherly-sisterly love

At times, Lord, they fight like cats.

But for now, they're romping together.
Playfully fighting.
Giggling and laughing.
Enjoying each other's company
as you intended.

Thanks, Lord Jesus,
for the closeness of family ties,
> for the time to relax together,
> for acceptance and understanding,
> for happiness and joy. Amen.

Teenage years

Teenage years are often turbulent years, Lord —
for teenagers and their parents!
But they're also years of incredible growth:
physically, emotionally,
sexually, intellectually.
Lord, give a willingness to learn
to these young people,
and to their mums and dads.

Let there be discussions
that are open and honest;
let there be the joy and exhilaration of success;
let there be the sadness and comfort of failure;
let there be boundaries
understood and accepted
under your guidance —
for teenagers exploring,
and for parents letting go.

And in all this, Jesus,
help us to remember that
you, too, were once a teenager! Amen.

Those considering marriage

God, who created man for woman,
and woman for man,*
be with us as we consider our future together.

This is a big decision we have to make, Lord.
Guide us as we work through the various issues
that will affect each of us,
and not only us,
but our friends and family,
our work commitments
and social engagements.
Give us wisdom to see
the changes that will occur,
and patience to cope with these changes.

Allow us to experience joy and happiness
as we plan for the wedding
and a new life together.
Teach us to trust in you,
and to place our confidence in you,
when making this decision
to be partners for life,
and in all our decisions that will follow.

God of relationships,
we thank you for each other,
and ask for your presence in our lives.
In Jesus' name. Amen.

* Genesis 2:21–24

Thanksgiving at a wedding anniversary

Lord God, thanks for the gift of marriage.
Today, especially,
I thank you for the ____ years of marriage
that you have allowed ____ and ____ to share.

Thanks for the gift of joy experienced
at the birth of a child,
and on significant occasions in the family life.

Thanks for the gift of companionship,
the sharing that is only possible
when two people know each other closely.

Thanks for the gift of forgiveness —
ever-present to restore
when a sharp word was spoken,
when kindness was lacking,
when love was briefly hidden.

Thanks for the gift of health restored
when illness struck,
and for your gift of health at all other times.

Thanks for your gift of comfort
when feelings were downcast,
when times were low,
and for raising this couple up
to experience your presence again.

Thanks, Lord, for the many blessings bestowed
on this couple.
Continue to be present in their life together,
and in the lives of all married couples and families.
In Jesus' name. Amen.

For a wedding anniversary of parents

It seems a long time
that Mum and Dad have been married, Lord —
at least to me!
Thanks, Lord, for the love and support
of husband and wife
for each other over the years.

Let their promise made to each other,
their willingness to give
and forgive,
their acceptance of each other,
their understanding when troubles come,
their support in times of crisis,
live on in me and my children. Amen.

At the breakdown of a relationship

Lord Jesus, do you know how I feel?
Have you felt the pain
that now tears at my very being?
Were you rejected like this?

Lord, I am hurting so!
My thoughts and feelings seem
as if they've been ambushed,
and are all over the place.
Calm me, Lord, comfort me.
Help me to collect myself.
Remind me that you were indeed rejected —
by Judas, by the mockers and the taunters . . .
even by me, Lord!

As you felt pain,
let me feel my pain with you.
As you were rejected,
let me hand my rejections over to you.
As you were hurt,
let my hurting find rest in you.

Lord Jesus, you do know how I feel.
Restore me in your love.
Give me courage to start again
with your presence.
Let all my relationships be based on
your relationship with me.
In your name I pray. Amen.

Prayers for mothers

Appreciation of our mothers

Lord, you cared for your mother,
even when you were dying.*
Give us the same appreciation of,
and dedication to, our mothers. Amen.

* John 19:26,27

For those who gave birth to us

Lord, we praise and thank you
for those who brought us into this world.
For some it was a joyful occasion;
for some it was painful — physically,
and even, for some — emotionally.
Yet, they still bore us.
We thank you for our mothers,
who gave birth to us. Amen.

For mothers who are no longer with us

Lord, for some of us,
our mothers have departed this life,
and are now with you.
We thank you for the treasured memories:
of home-cooked meals,
of loving acceptance
when we were rejected by others,
of family times
nurtured by Mum's guiding hand.
We thank you for the values and morals
instilled by our mothers,
which linger on in our lives, and now
affect the way we bring our own children up.
Amen.

For mothers of young children

Lord, our mums are part and parcel of our lives.
Give them patience and joy in dealing with us.

Thanks for their skills —
    in preparing our lunches,
    in listening to our concerns,
    in hurrying us up when we are loitering,
    in encouraging our music practices.

Help us to appreciate our mothers —
to ease their workloads
by doing our share around the house;
to make them happy
by positive attitudes and contributions
to our family life.

Thanks, Lord, for giving me a mother. Amen.

For mothers of grown-ups

Lord, I am now independent of my mother.
But she is still my mother.
Help me to respect her needs
as she grows older.
Allow us to talk together as adults.
Let us share together experiences
which enrich the lives of both of us.
Lord, as she grows older,
help me to do for her, as I am able,
what she has done for me.
Thanks, Lord, for my mother. Amen.

For mothers who have lost a child

Lord, we think of those mothers
who have lost a child;
who perhaps feel they have been robbed
of the right to see their
child grow and blossom and mature.
Comfort them, Lord God.

As a Father, you saw your Son die
when everything seemed to be before him,
but in his dying everything was achieved
that you set out for him.

Comfort those mothers who mourn.
Let them know that in their child's dying
all that was planned
for their child in this world
has been accomplished.

Let them know, Lord, that in you
their role of mother was not in vain,
but in the time they had as a mother
they served you in mothering their child
and gave you praise. Amen.

For all who are mothers

Lord, we thank you
    for all who have been mothers,
    for all who are mothers now,
    for all who will be mothers in years to come.

May they receive joy and pleasure
in their mothering,
and may we respect and honour them
as they give praise to you. Amen.

Prayers for fathers

A father of young children

Lord, give me energy and enthusiasm
    for my children's games;
give me time to listen
    to their experiences and stories;
give me patience
    in teaching them right and wrong;
give me willingness
    to read and explore with them;
give me strength in supporting their mother;
give me love to share, in large measure. Amen.

Prayer of a father

Lord, help me to love the mother of our children.
Amen.

A busy father

Lord Jesus, be with those fathers
whose lives are ruled by work demands,
and business decisions,
and important discussions.
Help them to remember
that you have called them
to be fathers first, and businessmen second.
Allow them to remember that
time and love and presence
are much more valuable than
possessions and money and presents.
Lord God, mould them in your image. Amen.

On a birthday (an older male)

O God, birthdays mean different things
to different people.

On this day, Lord, I give thanks to you —
thanks for parents and family,
who shaped and moulded my early life;
thanks for friends — from school,
from activities I took part in as a youth,
from camps —
who accepted me,
and who, together with me, learnt and grew.

On this day, Lord, I give thanks to you —
thanks for my wife,
for her patience, love, and support;
for being the mother of the children
you have generously provided to us.
Thanks, Lord, for these children —
for the times of joy and adventure;
for the hard times we've had to work through;
for the jigsaws and games;
and bike rides and stories we've shared.

On this day, Lord, I give thanks to you —
thanks for adult friends,
for those who've moved on
in different directions;
for those who've wandered into my life
through changing states and jobs;
for those who've supported,
and advised,

and challenged,
and shared,
so that we could do together
what we couldn't do apart.

Thanks, God, for the different people
and different activities
that have made up my life. Amen.

A reflection on times ahead

Lord of the past,
thanks for the blessings you have given.
Lord of the present, be with me now.
Lord of the future, guide my steps in your ways.

Allow me to use the experience and knowledge
I have gained for the benefit
of my family, my friends,
those with whom I can share the good news.
Give me wisdom —
so that I may be wise!
Not in the wisdom of the world,
but in my dealings with people,
so that I may advise sensibly,
abitrate judiciously,
support regularly,
encourage frequently,
challenge always.

Allow me to continue to grow
in experience and knowledge —
never to sit back on my laurels,

but to consider every viewpoint,
and to go forward in faith,
trusting in your guidance. Amen.

Thanks, Lord, for life,
and for life eternal. Amen.

Before an operation

Dear Lord, you are the great physician,
the healer of men and women.
Be with me today as I undergo this operation.
My emotions are a little mixed.
There's fear of the unknown,
and hope for the future.
There's concern if something goes wrong,
and confidence in the skills of the surgeons.
Be with me, Lord;
lay your protective hand over me,
and allow me to accept
your will for my life. Amen.

Lord, I thank you for the gift of healing
you share with your people:
for the skill of the surgeon,
the quiet words of the anaesthetist,
the reassurance of the sister.
I thank you, Lord,
for the care of the nurse,
for the challenge of the physiotherapist,
for the company of fellow sufferers.
Lord, let them use their gifts to your glory,
and for the good of all people. Amen.

After an operation

Thanks, Lord, for keeping me safe.
Thanks that the pain is eased in so many ways —
through pain killers,
through care and skill,
through words of support,
through the one who picks me up
from the hospital.
Lord Jesus,
help me and help others to look forward
to that time when there will be no more pain.*
Amen.

* Revelation 21:1–5

Death

Unexpected death

Death comes so unexpectedly, Lord.
Just when we had things going smoothly,
and there were great plans in the air.
Suddenly. It's stopped.
No more. A complete change of direction.
Lord, at this time,
help us to grasp your promises.
Cut down, but a new start.
An ending, and a beginning.
Darkness, but your light.
Death, and yet life.
As we look back in sadness,
help us look forward in joy.
In your name. Amen.

A cry from the heart (1)

Well, what is life, Lord,
but an opportunity for death to come?
And yet, in the midst of our despair,
I know it is much more: a gift from you —
to be moulded, and used as you see fit;
to be influenced,
and to have influence for the common good;
to train and encourage and challenge others;
to be taken, when and where you decide.
Help me not to waste
the opportunities given to me,
but to seize the moments,
and to put all my energy and creativity
into each situation I am placed in;
so when my time comes,
may I look back and know
that you, God, lived in me,
and I lived in you. Amen.

A cry from the heart (2)

Living Lord Jesus,
take my pain and hurt,
enfold your arms around me and my family.
Let each of us know that your mercies
are new every morning.*

As I have died in you,
take my fear of death,
and replace it with your love and compassion,
your comfort and presence. Amen.

* Lamentations 3:22,23

On the death of a parent (1)

Lord of life, and Lord of death,
we thank you for being in control.

At this time of sadness, Lord God,
we ask that your Holy Spirit
would move among us like a gentle breeze,
so that we may hand our concerns,
our worries, our doubts,
our grief, our sadness to you.
And, in doing so,
may we receive from you
a large measure of your comfort
and reassurance.

Lord God, you have experienced the pain
of the death of a son.
Stand by us now, as we experience the pain
of the death of our parent. Amen.

On the death of a parent (2)

We give you thanks, Lord,
for a life lived to the full —
for a life which reflected your love;
for a life which enjoyed
the gifts of your world,
and used them for service and fellowship,
for family and friends,
for work and recreation;
for a life which knew that true life is in you.
In Jesus' name. Amen.

The death of a mother

> *Those who trust in the Lord for help*
> *will find their strength renewed.*
> *They will rise on wings like eagles;*
> *they will run and not get weary;*
> *they will walk and not grow weak.*
> Isaiah 40:31 (TEV)

Lord God, the words of your prophet Isaiah
sum up Mum's attitude.
Simply: she trusted in you.
So often, when she was weak,
she found her strength renewed —
because she trusted in you.
So often, when it seemed she could only crawl,
she rose up on wings like eagles —
because she trusted in you.
So often, when it seemed
there was nothing but tiredness left,
her trust in you allowed her to run again.

Lord, when we are weak,
when we are weary,
when we feel our strength is gone,
remind us of our mother,
and her trust in you for help.
Allow us the privilege
of trusting in you in that way.
In Jesus' name. Amen.

God's care for me

God, as you cared so much
that you gave attention to
every intimate detail of creation,*
care for me
with attention greater than I can know,
yet so close that I can feel your breath,
and in your caring,
free me to care. Amen.

* Genesis 1:9–31

Leisure and relaxation

God worked six days, then blessed the seventh. These prayers celebrate the blessing of leisure and relaxation.

Time off

Thanks, Lord, for days
when I can forget the pressures of work.
Help me to remember your model
of six days of work, and one of rest.*
Teach me to achieve what I can
in my working hours,
and when I have done my best
to relax and rest,
giving praise to you
for what has been accomplished
and allowing my body and mind to recuperate.
Amen.

* Genesis 2:1–3

Sleep

Overnight

Thanks, Lord, for the quiet of the night.
Give me a peaceful sleep
that I may wake refreshed
and ready to face the rigours of the new day.
May I be sensible in my sleeping habits,
using this gift of rest wisely,
so that my waking hours
may be spent in useful activity. Amen.

Afternoon snooze

Lord, I think those countries
that have an afternoon siesta
have got it right.
Thanks for the occasions
when I can fit in an afternoon snooze,
and be refreshed in this way.
May I praise you in my sleeping
and my waking. Amen.

A walk in the park

Thanks for the green of the grass, Lord,
the blue of the sky overhead,
the brown of the trees,
and the brightness of the sunshine.
Thanks for the colours
the people around me are wearing,
and for the different tones of their skin.
The peacefulness and harmony in this park
remind me that all people and activities
have their source in you.
As the walk in this park has delighted me,
so, Lord, let my life bring delight to you
and joy to those around me. Amen.

Jogging

Thanks for the benefits of jogging, Lord.
Be with all those who jog for whatever reason.

I enjoy their expressions:
the exhilaration of the man
with the spring in his step;
the pain of the person
trying to run that bit faster;
the thoughtfulness of the woman
attempting to move to
another level of fitness;
the satisfaction of the one
who's just run a personal best;
the pleasure of the family
spending time together.

Through their efforts, Lord, allow them to gain
not only physical fitness,
but emotional and spiritual wellbeing as well.
Amen.

Participating in sporting activities

Lord Jesus, let all people realise the benefits
of taking part in sport.

Give direction and a sense of purpose
to those who are involved
at a high level of achievement.
Help them always to keep in mind
their aims and goals.
Prevent them from losing sight

of the pleasure motive
simply because of the pressures of winning.

And be with those who play sport
just for the fun of it.
Allow them to experience pleasant times
with their friends,
gain a level of fitness that is useful to them,
relax enough so that they can return
to their daily tasks refreshed,
and value the experience of unwinding.
In Jesus' name. Amen.

Watching sporting activities

Thanks, Lord,
for the wide coverage of sport on TV.
Make me sensible in the amount of time
I spend watching this. Amen.

Thanks, Lord, for the pleasure
of watching young athletes in action.
Help me to rejoice
in the gift of health and fitness
you have given to these people.
Allow me to speak words
of encouragement and support
to competitors and coaches.
May we together exhibit principles
of watching and participating
that bring a positive message to the community.
In your name. Amen.

Family time

Lord, teach us to make time
    to romp with the children,
    to give piggyback rides, and whirligigs,
    to throw the ball and kick the footy,
    to enjoy the simple things of life,
    to spend time together as a family. Amen.

Board games

For the variety of board games,
I thank you, Lord Jesus:
for the intricacies of chess,
for the simpleness of Ludo,
for the challenge of backgammon,
for the artistry of Pictionary,
for the mind-stretching that Scrabble causes,
for the tension of Monopoly.
For the joys and frustrations,
the good times and relaxation of board games,
I thank you, Lord Jesus. Amen.

Card games

Lord, whoever invented cards
knew what they were doing.
Thank you for their creative abilities.

Card games can be simple,
and they can be complex.
They can be played by the very young,
by the very old,
and by the very in-between!
Cards can be thought-provoking, and relaxing;
they can bring good family times,
and result in arguments.

Lord, whenever I play cards, may I do so fairly,
enjoying the fellowship,
and revelling in the competition. Amen.

Outdoor games

Thanks, Lord, for the outdoors:
> for grass to run on,
> for space to play,
> for seesaws and swings,
> for activities that everyone can join in,
> for life in all its fullness. Amen.

Music

Lord of miracles,
thanks for the miracle of music.
Tune our hearts to your song. Amen.

On musical tastes

It never ceases to make me wonder, God!
How will you provide for diverse musical tastes
in heaven?

Will the opera buff and the rock fan
sing together?
Will the country and western singer
and the jazz virtuoso
meet on common ground?
Will the power of the classical
overwhelm the simplicity of the folk?
Will dance music
compete with gospel singers for attention?
Will rap walk down the middle-of-the-road?

Creator of all things musical,
we praise you for diversity,
and look forward to the harmony
you will bring. Amen.

For the gift of music

Thanks, God,
    for voices to sing,
    instruments to play,
    tunes to compose,
    notes to combine.

Help us to use these
    to give pleasure and to praise you. Amen.

For the gifts of musical instruments

Thank you, Lord,
    for the creative abilities
    of makers of musical instruments.

Thank you, Lord,
    for the piano and its rich tones,
    for the guitar and its versatility,
    for the flute and its vibrant melody,
    for the drum and its lively rhythm,
    for the violin and its poignant moments,
    for the trumpet and its bold call,
    for the recorder and its simple tunes,
    for the tambourine and its joyful beat.

For these
and the most amazing variety of instruments,
I give you praise, Lord. Amen.

Enjoying a meal together

Thanks, Lord, for the company of friends
and the company of strangers.
Thank you for food and drink to enjoy.
As we share in celebration, and family times,
feasts and simple meals,
I give you thanks
for the generosity of your creation,
the thoughtfulness of those who invite us out,
the opportunities that time and money bring,
and the chances to practise hospitality.
In your name. Amen.

Going to the movies

The big screen excites, Lord.
The booming sound and amazing scenery
join together to lighten my heart.

Thank you, God, for fantasy and imagination,
for colour and sound,
for actresses and actors,
for storylines, and jokes,
for thought-provoking scenes
and dramatic action,
for humour and drama,
for pathos and humanity.

Lord, give writers, directors, and producers
discernment, honesty, and high moral values.
In your name, Jesus. Amen.

Reading (1)

So many books and magazines and newspapers!
Thanks for the ability to read, Lord Jesus.
May I be choosy in what I read,
and willing to share the knowledge I gain
in a humble manner.
Thanks for libraries, Lord,
where I can browse and borrow
to my heart's content.

I ask that you would be with the illiterate
in our land and overseas.
Be with those who are teaching others to read.
Thank you that so often it is your word
that is used to teach them the joy of reading,
and the truth about life. Amen.

Reading (2)

Just as I make time to read
my preferred sections of the newspaper,
a favourite book,
and magazines that deal with my interests,
teach me, Lord Jesus,
to make time to read the Scriptures,
that in them I might find life,
and come to you!* Amen.

* John 4:39

Gardening

So many people enjoy gardening, Lord.
How great and wise you are to have provided
such a simple hobby
that brings pleasure to so many.

Thanks for the variety of gardens:
the flowerbeds,
the immaculate lawns,
the vegetable patch,
the fruit-bearing trees,
the native bushes and trees,
the ornamentals.
As I garden,
may I be mindful of your presence;
may I tend the patch of land
I can work in with diligence;
may I take care of your creation
in what I do, and in what I use;
may I be in harmony with nature,
and so be in harmony with you.

O Lord, your creation is so magnificent.
I praise your name. Amen.

Nature

The gifts of God's creation astound, enthuse, and provide opportunity for relaxation and reflection. They also remind us that God is God.

The black cockatoo

The flight of the black cockatoo
astounds me.
Lord, help me to fly in my thoughts
and dreams and ideals. Amen.

Insects

God of all creatures,
help us to see that insects
are much more than creepy-crawlies —
that they are, in fact,
an important part of the planet
that they — and we — inhabit! Amen.

Scavengers!

The seagulls gathered as we ate
our sandwiches in the park.
Is there a better way to describe them
than — scavengers?

Thanks, Provider of life, for humble food.
Help us to be generous
in our thoughts and actions
toward those who have no choice
but to be scavengers to survive. Amen.

Blowflies

Blowflies!
Sometimes I wonder, God —
and yet, you work for good in all things.*
Let me see your good
in all that annoys me,
in all that seems to have no value,
in all that I wonder about.
Wonderful God, fill me with your wonder! Amen.

* Romans 8:28

Plants

Creator God,
where did you find the time
to create so many varieties of plants?
The trees, the bushes, the flowers all mingle
to provide an exhilarating sight,
and to give praise to you.

Help us to join together with them,
and with each other, to praise you. Amen.

The night sky

I join with the psalmist in praising you:
How clearly the sky reveals God's glory!*
The milky way is so clear;
the stars are so bright, and so many.
Thank you, Lord God,
for the open skies of your creation. Amen.

* Psalm 19:1

Hills

Thanks, Lord, for the smooth, rolling hills
that evoke different images.
Thanks, Lord of creation, for undulating hills
which bring relaxation
into the minds of travellers. Amen.

Wide-open spaces of the beach

Lord, I enjoy walking along the beach.
At low tide, there is lots of sand exposed,
and colourful shells,
with a backdrop of sandhills.

The beach is big enough to cope with all sorts
of people and groups:
a primary school having picnic races,
teenagers learning to surf,
fishermen collecting worms,
dogs running everywhere —
and still there is space and more . . .

Thanks, God,
for the wide expanses of this land. Amen.

Weather

Thanks, Lord, for sunshine,
for days when we can soak up
the warmth of the rays
and rejoice in all you have made.

Thanks, Lord, for rain
without which nothing would grow;
for the soft pitter-patter on the tin roof;
for the driving force of storms that leave the
earth refreshed and the roads clean.

Thanks, Lord, for wind
which helps to dry clothes;
which blows away the pollution we create;
which reminds us of your Spirit.

Thanks, Lord, for clouds,
for the amazing shapes that tease
and challenge our creativity;
for the protection they provide
from the hot summer sun.

Thanks, Lord, that you control the weather.
Amen.

Seasons of the year (in southern Australia)

Autumn

Thanks, Lord, for still warm days;
for soft refreshing rains
after the dryness of summer.
Thanks for the colours of the falling leaves,
and the carpets crunching and crinkling
under children's feet. Amen.

Winter

The cold chill air reaches into my bones,
making me shiver,
realising the need for warmth.
Thanks, God, for fires and heaters and energy,
for jumpers and skivvies and warm clothing.
Be with those who have to survive
in the harshness
of an outdoor winter. Amen.

Spring

The warming rays of the sun,
the new shoots of plants,
the grass looking greener and growing faster —
new life everywhere!
Jesus, Lord of life,
bring new life into our hearts
and into our relationships. Amen.

Summer

The beach, the barbecue, the sunburn!
Help us, Lord, to be sensible
as we take advantage of the
outdoor opportunities you give to us.

Thanks, Lord, for seasons;
thanks for differing perspectives on life. Amen.

An autumn day

Today, Lord, is a beautiful autumn day —
the sort of day that appears
in tourist advertisements for tropical islands.
Thanks, Lord, that your creative power
extends over all creation. Amen.

A winter's day

The rain is pelting down, Jesus.
Some people, God of creation, describe this day
as a miserable day!
Develop their narrow views.

And it's cold!
Thanks for the warmth of clothes and heaters.
Make us wise in our use of them.

And the cloud cover is thick!
Remind us of your presence
in the clouds, Lord God. Amen.*

* Exodus 19:9,16–20

The wind chills my bones, Lord,
but I've got warm clothes and coats
and rooms to shelter in, and heaters.

Lord, be with those
who have to sleep out tonight,
who have nothing but the clothes
they are wearing;
who will line up for some warm soup,
and use an old newspaper as a blanket.
Wrap them in your warmth, Lord.

Bless the efforts of the emergency shelters;
and the workers who give up the warmth
of their home
to seek out these people,
and reassure them they have worth.

Challenge me, Lord, to support this work,
through my prayers, and my financial support,
and my presence.

Lord, you know what it was like
to be homeless.
Let your love and care rest on the homeless
in our town tonight. Amen.

A spring day

Lord, I can almost see and hear
the grass growing
in response to the warmth of the sunshine
after the heavy rains.
Help me to grow in the warmth of your love.
Amen.

The weather at this time of year
can be so fickle, Lord.
As each day, and, sometimes, even each hour,
brings different weather,
remind me that you are the constant
behind all changes. Amen.

A summer's day

Well, it's hot today, Lord, and I'm sweltering.
But I thank you for the availability
of beaches and pools,
the shade of the huge trees,
and the cool of the evening.
May I not hide from you
in any of these places.* Amen.

* Genesis 3:8

General

We can communicate with God at any time, in a variety of places, in different situations, about all sorts of things. These prayers lead us to do just that.

Prayers during the day

While these prayers were written in the countryside, and during holiday time, they could be prayed anywhere in any season.

Dawn

Thanks, Lord, for the stillness
of the early morning. Amen.

As the breeze rustles through the leaves,
and the birds begin their calls,
I am reminded, O Lord, of the way
your Holy Spirit gently moves me. Amen.

Sunrise

The first rays of the sun
bring warmth and light.
Allow me, Creator God,
to bring warmth and light
to those I meet today. Amen.

Breakfast

For food to replenish us,
and give us strength for the day ahead;
for fellowship,
and the sharing of hopes and dreams;
for talk,
and being accepted in what we say;
we give you thanks, Lord Jesus Christ. Amen.

Mid-morning

It's quiet in the house, Lord,
and the children are out exploring.
That gives me a chance to reflect.
Make me quiet in your presence, Lord Jesus.
Amen.

Lunchtime

Thanks, Lord Jesus, for the chance to pause;
thanks for food that strengthens,
and drink that refreshes;
and thanks for some time to myself. Amen.

Afternoons

Afternoons provide a chance
to catch up, Lord —
> to do the reading that is waiting;
> to write a letter;
> to visit a friend, or a stranger;
> to finish the job that won't wait any longer.

Good God,
guide me in my use of afternoon time. Amen.

Evening meal

Thanks, Lord, for the opportunity
to sit together as a family;
to share our excitements and sadnesses
from the day just done;
to commiserate, and offer support;
to laugh, and join in the exhilaration.
Bless our time of eating,
and our time of fellowship, Lord. Amen.

Dusk

Seeing the superb blue wren
and the scarlet robin
reminds me, Lord God, that they
praise you with their colour, and their song.

Encourage me to use
the attributes you have endowed me with
to praise you. Amen.

Nightfall

As darkness comes,
the trees slowly become
shadows silhouetted against the sky.
They lose their distinctiveness, God,
and blend into the darkness.
Help us to blend in with your family, God,
but to be confident enough in you
to serve in our individual ways. Amen.

Darkness

Darkness is rapidly falling, Lord,
replacing the light; Jesus, let your light
shine brightly into our darkness. Amen.

End of the day

The stillness envelops us;
Lord Jesus Christ, let your blessing rest
on our stillness tonight. Amen.

Thanks for caring for us

We thank you, Jesus, that you came to care —
that you brought light into darkness,
that you shared grace and truth
and blessed us with your blessing.*

We thank you, Jesus, that you care for us now
through our friends
with their silent, but understanding, listening,

with their words of encouragement,
with their supportive actions,
with their comforting touch.

Teach us, O Lord, to care
as you cared for us
on the cross
and in our daily lives. Amen.

* John 1:4,16,17

Thanks for support

You are present, Lord,
in your people.

Words of support and words of encouragement
mean a lot;
being able to express concerns to others,
and hearing a sympathetic comment
bring comfort.

For the encouraging word,
for the offer of help,
for the sharing of concern,
for the understanding comment,
thanks, Lord.

Help me to remember
that you are present
in your people. Amen.

A prayer when frustrated

God, where are you?
It seems that many people are against me.
They don't understand my words,
they treat my concerns lightly.
They want me to be someone that isn't me.

Lord, help me to be me.
Help me to remember I am made in your image.
Let me recognise that what I am,
that what I have, is given by you,
and so is special, is important, has worth.

Lord, in your sight I am worthy.
Give me confidence to share that worth;
to let others see what you have given me,
to encourage others to see
what you have given them.

And help us, together, to praise your name.
Amen.

Friends

Thanks, Lord, for friends.

For friends of long ago —
who have now moved away,
or whom we have moved away from.

For friends of long standing
who have opened their hearts and homes to us,
with whom we have been able to share
our joys and sorrows.

For friends who have welcomed us to
the area where we now live,
who have helped us to settle
in this community,
who have made it easier
in finding our way round.

For new friends,
who challenge us
with their thinking and ideas.

For family, who are not just family,
but over the years have become friends too.
For those in my workplace
who accept me as I am,
and offer the hand of friendship.

Lord Jesus, my greatest friend,
help me to be a friend to all these
and to others too,
who perhaps have to search for a friend,
who perhaps don't know the joy
or intimacy of true friendship. Amen.

People we meet on holidays

Thanks, Lord,
for the friendliness and helpfulness
of those strangers we met on holidays.
Thanks for the local knowledge
they were willing to share,
which turned ordinary occasions
into times of interest,
and mundane experiences
into educational events.

In our lives,
help us to be friendly and willing to share,
so that ordinary lives
may become extraordinary.

As you have befriended me, Lord,
so inspire me to befriend others. Amen.

Simple lives

Thanks, Lord, for those who live simple lives,
and serve others by sharing what they do best;
like an old lady I saw in a garden,
where bantams were exploring,
controlling the insects,
and plants growing wildly,
as nature intended.
Let that simpleness and naturalness
pervade our lives. Amen.

The country cemetery

A child once said:
'Not many people live in a cemetery, do they?'

It's true, Lord, not many people live here,
but the tombstones tell stories of long ago —
> of brave adventurous folk,
> of workers and settlers,
> of tragedies and young deaths,
> of large families and husbands and wives.

They live in our memory, Lord.
May they also live in you,
and may we have the privilege
of meeting them all one day. Amen.

Name-calling

I guess, Lord Jesus, in your days on earth,
particularly in the week of your passion,
you were called
many uncomplimentary names.

Forgive us when we abuse and hurt others
by using names that devalue those
who are made in your image.

Comfort those who suffer
because of unthinking insults,
arising from misuse of their name. Amen.

Names

Thanks, Lord Jesus, that you call me by name,
and you know who I am.*

Thanks that I can bear your name.
Help me to live up to it in word and deed.

Let me respect other people and their names,
and to use them, not in any derogatory way,
but to engender respect and self-esteem.

In your name, I pray. Amen.

* Psalm 139:1

Detours

Sometimes, God,
when travelling we take a detour.
Occasionally that means
we don't know exactly where we are going,
but eventually we join the main road again.
Lord, when we take detours
from the way you would have us travel,
keep your guiding hand on us,
and redirect us so that we may not be lost,
but found in you. Amen.

Long and winding roads

Long and winding roads take us here and there,
but eventually bring us
to where we are travelling:
the gate of a property,
or the door of a house.

Guide us, Lord God, director of the way,
that the long and winding roads
we choose to travel on,
may be the way you would have us go,
and may lead us to the gate you have opened*
and to the door of your love and life.
Amen.

* John 10:7–10

Lost and found

Lord, when we are feeling lost and lonely,
help us to see your arms stretching out to us.*
When we have turned away from you,
give us the courage to admit our wrong,
and to turn to you;
so, let us experience the joy of being found,
and of being in your presence at all times,
in Jesus' name. Amen.

* Luke 15

Pets

Thanks, Lord Jesus,
for the companionship of animals;
particularly for that favourite pet
that is faithful and loyal.
May I be a good owner,
and a worthy companion too. Amen.

Loss of a pet

Sometimes pets escape or die, Lord,
and it's not easy to handle this loss.

Yet even though I am sad,
make me glad for the enjoyable times
we had together.

Thanks for the privilege of looking
after one of your creatures.

Take care of my pet,
as you take care of me.* Amen.

* Matthew 6:26

SECTION 4

Blessings

To leave with a blessing is to go enriched. Whether the words are from God, or from a parent or friend, to be blessed is to depart with purpose and hope.

Feel free to change 'you' to 'us' or 'me' in these blessings, to make them more personal or appropriate for family and home use.

The blessing of the Triune God be with you.
Go with the peace of the Lord Jesus Christ,
the presence of the Holy Spirit,
and the protection of God the Father. Amen.

Take the promises of God with you:
    the promise of the Father's care,
    the promise of the Son's love and compassion,
    the promise of the Holy Spirit's presence.
Go into your day blessed
by the Father, Son, and Holy Spirit. Amen.

Go into the world,
singing praises to God,
taking the light of Christ with you,
sharing your faith with the world.
The blessing of the Father, Son, and Holy Spirit
rest on you. Amen.

Live as God's people;*
take his presence
into all the challenging situations
you find yourself in;
know and share his unique love;
go with the blessing
of Father, Son, and Holy Spirit. Amen.

* 1 Peter 2:9

God the Father care for you wherever you go;
God the Son lift you when you fall,
and carry you when you falter;
God the Holy Spirit strengthen you, renew you,
and free you to be his creation;
the blessing of Father, Son, and Holy Spirit
be with you. Amen.

Go with the blessing of God,
the God who calls you,*
and who sends you in his name. Amen.

* Isaiah 6:8

May the God of all truth
fill you with his truth and love.
Go with the blessing of God the Father,
in the presence of Jesus his Son,
by the power of the Holy Spirit.
The peace of God be with you. Amen.

An Advent blessing

The Lord Jesus come into your lives,
each day, and every day,
and make you his child. Amen.

For the Christmas season

Go with the peace of God the Father;
may this peace rule your life always.
Go with the love of Jesus;
may this love fill you as the waters fill the sea.
Go with the presence of the Holy Spirit;
may this presence
enliven and renew you each day. Amen.

A farewell blessing

The God of hellos and goodbyes
encourage you to reach out;
the God of old friends and new friends
fill you with anticipation;
the God of the past, present, and future
allow you a sense of vision. Amen.

The following blessings are from the Bible (TEV).

Numbers 6:24–26

May the Lord bless you and take care of you;
may the Lord be kind and gracious to you;
may the Lord look on you with favour
and give you peace. Amen.

Psalm 67:1,2,6b,7

God, be merciful to us and bless us;
look on us with kindness,
so that the whole world may know your will;
so that all nations may know your salvation.

God, our God, has blessed us.
God has blessed us;
may all people everywhere honour him. Amen.

Romans 15:13

May God, the source of hope,
fill you with all joy and peace
by means of your faith in him,
so that your hope will continue to grow
by the power of the Holy Spirit. Amen.

2 Corinthians 13:13

The grace of the Lord Jesus Christ,
the love of God,
and the fellowship of the Holy Spirit
be with you all. Amen.

Ephesians 6:23,24

May God the Father and the Lord Jesus Christ
give to all Christian people
peace and love with faith.
May God's grace be with all those who
love our Lord Jesus Christ with undying love.
Amen.

1 Thessalonians 5:23,24

May the God who gives us peace
make you holy in every way
and keep your whole being —
spirit, soul, and body —
free from every fault
at the coming of our Lord Jesus Christ.
He who calls you will do it,
because he is faithful. Amen.

2 Thessalonians 3:16

May the Lord himself,
who is our source of peace,
give you peace at all times and in every way.
The Lord be with you all. Amen.

Hebrews 13:21

May the God of peace
provide you with every good thing
you need in order to do his will,
and may he,
through Jesus Christ,
do in us what pleases him. Amen.

1 Peter 5:14b

May peace be with all of you
who belong to Christ. Amen.

2 Peter 3:18a

Continue to grow in the grace and knowledge
of our Lord and Saviour Jesus Christ. Amen.

Revelation 22:21

May the grace of the Lord Jesus
be with everyone. Amen.

Biblical Index

Genesis
1 61
1:2 36,63
1:9–31 137
1:26,27 31
2:1–3 138
2:21–24 120
3:8 15,156
Exodus
16:7 18
19:9,16–20 154
Numbers
6:24–26 173
Ezra
9:5,6a 17
Psalm
5:3 12
19:1 150
30:5 14
51:10 31
66:1–7 30
67:1,2,6,7 173
86:11 34
127:2 138
137:7–9 110
139 50
139:1 166
141:2 18
Isaiah
6:8 171
29:13 38
40 114
40:31 136

Lamentations
3:22,23 16,134
Ezekiel
37:1–14 36,54
Micah
6:8 23,39
Zechariah
14:7 19
Matthew
6:9 20–22
6:10 23,24
6:11 24
6:12 25
6:13 26,27
6:26 168
10:30,31 116
11:28–30 109
23:13–28 110
26:42 23
Mark
1:39 67
3:1 67
6:2 67
9:24 40
10:45 66
11:15–17 110
16:2 8
Luke
6:12 13
10:38–42 68
11:2 20–23
11:3 24
11:4 25–27

176

Reference	Page
15	167
18:9–14	41
24:5	53
24:29	11

John
Reference	Page
1:4	160
1:16	160
1:17	160
2:13–17	111
3:8	36
4:6	111
10:7–10	167
10:10	54
11:35	111
14:27	58
19:27	123
20:19	9
20:27,28	59
21:4	10
21:12	10

Romans
Reference	Page
8:28	150
15:13	173

2 Corinthians
Reference	Page
8:9	33
13:13	173

Galatians
Reference	Page
5:1,13–25	34
5:22	55–63

Ephesians
Reference	Page
5:1,2	31
6:23,24	174

1 Thessalonians
Reference	Page
5:23,24	174

2 Thessalonians
Reference	Page
3:16	174

Hebrews
Reference	Page
13:21	175

1 Peter
Reference	Page
2:9	171
5:14b	175

2 Peter
Reference	Page
3:18a	175

Revelation
Reference	Page
21:1–5	132
21:4	132
22:16	19
22:21	175

Topical index

abuse, verbal 165
activities, everyday 18
administration, church 64
Advent 47
advice of friends 37
anger 110
appreciation of
    mothers 123
attitude towards
    unemployed 77
autumn 153,154

babies 117
banners 73
baptism 43–46
beach 151
bearing Jesus' name 166
being open to Jesus 9
belonging to God
    28,30,31,66
Bible 147
bicycles 99
birth 116,117,124
blessing 39,160
blessings 170–175
books 147
business 77,79,82
busyness 109

call 171
cars 101
cards 143
care 30,49,132,137,160,
    168,170,171
    for animals 168
challenge 87,142
change 133,156
chaos 63
children 85,116,117,
    125,128
children's club 69
Christ
  Chosen One 32
  cross of 51
  light of 170
  love of 37
Christmas 48
church
  administration 64
  cleaning 70
  life 64–73
  seasons 47–54
  strangers 44
closeness to God 40
clouds 152
cold 153–155
comfort 36,78,114,126,
    134,135
committees 68
communication
    90–98,158
community 160
compassion 170
competition 141
computers 96,97
concern 131
confessing Jesus 10

counsel of Spirit 37
Counsellor 37
creation 30,31,102,143,
    154
creativity 145,146
criticism 108
cross of Christ 51,52

daily needs 24
darkness 160
dawn 157
day of the Lord 19
death 133–136
depression 114
destitute 149,153,155
detours 166
devil 27
discipline of prayer 13
dreams 149
driving, off-road 102

Easter 53
ecology 149
education 83–89
emotions 111,112
empathy of Jesus 122,134,
    135,137
encouragement 37,85,95,
    161
energy of children 117
Epiphany 49
eternal life 53,131
eternity 31
ethics 77
evening 9,11,13,15,
    17–19

everyday activities 18
evil 27
excitement 117
experience in life 129

faith 40,174
faithfulness 44,62
family 62,125,128,142,
    159
  Christian 35,46
farewell 172
father 20,21,128
Father, God the 20,21,
    30,31,128
feelings 122
fellowship 65,143,158,
    159,173
fitness 140,141
flowers 72
food 146,158
forgiveness 25,41
free time 107
freedom 34,41
  of will 23
friends 163,164
fruits of Spirit 17,55–63
frustration 162
future 79,172

games 142,143
gardening 148
general prayers 157–
    168
generosity 24
getting away from it all
    102

gifts of God 145
giving self 41,121,122
glory of the Lord, 18
God,
  belonging to 28,30,
    31,66
  care of 30,171
  gifts of 121
  goodness of 24,61,
    150
  guidance of 11,129
  help of 26,110
  hiding from 156
  image of 31,128,162
  in control 30,32
  invitation of 41
  kingdom of 23,35
  knowing 31
  love of 20,156
  praise of 150,159
  presence of 15,34,40,
    154,161
  renewing me 40
  relying on 26
  seeking us 15,41
  trusting in 120,136
  will of 23
  with me 34
Good Friday 52
good news 49
goodness 24,61,150
  of God 24,61,150
grace 173–175
grieving 133–136

growth 156
guidance of God 11,129

heat 156
heaven 22
help of God 26,110
helpers 38
hiding from God 156
high school students 86
hills 151
history 165
holidays 164
holiness 174
Holy Spirit (*see also*
  Spirit) 44,157
homeless 149,153,155
honesty 38,77,79,119
hope 79,173
hospitality 146
human elements 42,46
humanity of Jesus 32
humility 17,62,63

ideals 149
illiterate, the 147
image of God 31,128,162
individuality 160
insects 149
instruments, musical 145
insults 165
intelligence 96
invention 97
invitation of God 41
involvement in
  worship 67

Jesus 32,33,63,160,165
  coming into our lives 8,33,172
  empathy of 122,134, 135,137
  friend 163
  glory of 98
  light 19,160
  Lord 28,49,50
  love 40
  name of 166
  peace in 58,59
  presence of 10,47,158, 171
  Saviour 33
jogging 140
joy 57,117,173
justice 79

kindness 60
kingdom of God 23,35
knowing God 31
knowledge 175

ladies' fellowship 68
land, loss of 78,79
learning 34,65,83–89
leaves 153
leisure 138–148
letter-writing 90,91
life, living 8,12,23,28,33, 36,42,53,66,89,116–137,147,153,172
lifestages 116–137
light, Jesus as 19,160

lonely 167
Lord 18,28,38,50,173
Lord's Prayer 20–29
loss of land 75–79
lost 166,167
love 20,40,55,156, 171–174

mail 91
majesty 32
marriage 120–122
mental health 107–114
mercy 173
miracles 42,100,116,144
morality 146
morning 8,10,12,14,16,18, 19
mothers 123–127
motor cars 101
motorbikes 103
movies 146
music 94,144,145

name-calling 165
names 166
  of God 30–37
nature 139,148–156, 159,160,164
needs, daily 24
neighbourliness 95
new beginnings 16
newspapers 95,96

occupations 80
off-road driving 102

openness 119
open to Jesus 9
opportunities 59,134
organisation 64,69
our Father 20,21
outdoors, the 143,154

parts of the body 116
pastor 38,44
pain, no more 132
patience 59,117
peace 9,12,35,58,59
pets 168
plants 150
power
  of God 30
  of Holy Spirit 44,171
praise 145,150,159,170
prayer, praying 13,29
preparation 38,44,125
presence of God, Jesus,
  Holy Spirit 10,15,16,
  34,37,38,40,44,47,
  50,155,158,161,
  170–172
pressure 109
price paid by Jesus 33
pride (and humility) 17
pride in work 76
priorities 128
privilege 116
promises 170
protection 11,131,170
provision 24,175
pushbikes 99

quiet 157,158,160

radio 94,95
rain 152
reading 147
reassurance 135
recognising Jesus 10
rejoicing 14
relationships 35,118,119,
  120,122,157
relaxation 106,107,112,
  138–148,158
relying on God 26
remembering 46,165
renewal (by God) 31,40,
  44,54
research 87
respect for other road
  users 103
responsible reporting
  (papers, TV etc) 96
responsibility 34,103,116
rest 11,14,112,138,139,160
resurrection 53
righteous anger 110

sadness 133
safety 99
Saviour 33
schooling, stages of 84
seasons of the year
  153–156
seeking Jesus 8
self 27
self-control 63
selfish anger 110

self-worth 162
senses, the 18
sent by God 171
serving others 91,164
serving God 175
sharing 49,149,159,171
ships 104
simple things of life 142, 164
sin 25
skills 132
sky 150
sleep 138
speaking 91,161
Spirit,
   in us 39
   being led by 36
   counsel of 37
   filled with 36
   fruits of 17,55–63
   presence of 37,170,172
sport 140,141
spring 153,156
stages of life 116–137
standards 95
steam trains 106
stewardship 79
stillness 114
strangers 44,146
stress 113
structures
   organisational 71
students, high school 86
study 87,88
summer 154,156

suffering 48
Sunday school 69
sun 152
sunrise 157
support 45

talking 91
teachers,
   teaching 83,85,86
teenage years 119
telephones 92
television 93,141
temptation 26
thanks,
   for bikes 99
   for children 116
   for cleaners 70
   for creation 150
   for family, friends 129
   for ladies' fellowship 68
   for learning 87
   for life 117,131
   for love shown 55,132
   for marriage 121
   for mothers 123–127
   for music 144,145
   for plane flight attendants 100
   for ships 105
   for skills 132
   for support 111
   for walking 102
   for work 76

for worship 39
to God 79

time together (as a
    family) 142
time, use of 102,113,159
tolerance 94
transport 99–106
travel 82,167
truck drivers 104
trusting in God 120,136
truth 171

unemployed 81
  attitude towards 77
unity 41,42
ushers 71

variety 80,88,94,142,144
verbal abuse 165

wages, use of 76
walking 102
water 46
Way, the 167
weariness 14
weather 152
welcoming 72
wide-open spaces 151
will
  freedom of 23
  of God 24
wind 152
winter 153,154,155
witnessing 170,171,173
Word, the 38

words of
    encouragement 95
work 76–82
  those out of 77,81
world, temptations of 26
worship 38–46,67
writing letters 90,91